OUR 2ND AMERICAN REVOLUTION

HONORING THE SACRIFICES OF OUR FOUNDERS

"Let's All Be Patriots and Keep America Free"

WILLIAM E. SHUTTLEWORTH

WESTBOW
PRESS

WestBow Press books may be ordered through booksellers or by contacting:

WestBow Press
A Division of Thomas Nelson
1663 Liberty Drive
Bloomington, IN 47403
www.westbowpress.com
1-(866) 928-1240

ISBN: 978-1-4497-0177-2 (sc)
ISBN: 978-1-4497-0175-8 (e)
ISBN: 978-1-4497-0178-9 (hc)

Library of Congress Control Number: 2010926331

Printed in the United States of America

WestBow Press rev. date: 05/11/2012

Endorsements and Praise for
Our 2nd American Revolution

To: All Americans who are concerned about our nation's future
Re: *Our 2nd American Revolution* by William E. Shuttleworth

*"Finally, a work that truly addresses the real issues that confront our nation! **Our 2nd American Revolution** by William Shuttleworth is written for the "common man" in an enjoyable and easy-to-read format. This book describes how **'We the People'** have strayed far away from the form of government that our founding fathers originally created for us in 1787. But Shuttleworth does not stop there. He also provides answers and precisely explains what **'We the People'** must do to return to the fundamental principles of the U.S. Constitution. This is a real 'page-turner' from the beginning of the book to the rear cover! If you, like me, are an American Patriot and have become frustrated with where our nation is headed, do yourself a favor and read this book."*

—**William J. Couch,** Retired Indiana School
Superintendent and U.S. Government Teacher

Re: *Our 2nd American Revolution* by William E. Shuttleworth

*"Town hall meetings with passionate and concerned Americans are eerily reminiscent of the unrest in the 1700s when the founders of our country took bold steps to write a Constitution for the United States of America. **Our 2nd American Revolution** makes the case that it is time to revert to the simple basic form of **'We the People'** government that was envisioned by our founders. An easy read with numerous quotes and references from icons of democracy, the author leads the reader through the derailment of our government and then proposes that we take our country back by proposing nine specific goals of the second American Revolution. At the top of the list is a call for the removal of as many of the 535 elected incumbent members of the U.S. Congress as is possible in November of 2010. "**Our 2nd American Revolution** is a timely and important read that I can easily recommend ..."*

—**David L. Daugherty,** The Daugherty Companies, Inc.

For additional copies of this book:

Visit the book's website:
http://our2ndamericanrevolution.com
or http://oursecondamericanrevolution.com
or visit any online retailer such as www.amazon.com
or www.barnesandnoble.com

You may email the author at: thebook@goteaparty.us

DEDICATION

It is customary for authors to dedicate their book to certain people who have in some way inspired or influenced them. This task is easy for the author of <u>Our Second American Revolution</u>. There can be no more fitting dedication for this book than to dedicate it to each and every one of the founding fathers of the United States. The contributions our founders made for not just America but quite literally the entire world are beyond our ability to measure or to comprehend. In W. Cleon Skousen's book *The 5000 Year Leap*, he describes how the civilization of the entire world had advanced five thousand years in a period of just two hundred years and that this advancement was primarily driven by the formation of America under the leadership of our founding fathers. Skousen's book is a great read and one that any serious student of history should own. Our founders created for us a nation that contained an environment of Freedom and Liberty under which capitalism and free enterprise could flourish unencumbered or held back in any way by an overreaching or tyrannical government. The result was a period of growth and prosperity that was literally a worldwide miracle and a phenomenon that had never occurred before and has had no rival since.

My primary goal when conducting the research for this book was to study America's unique history in an attempt to understand what our founding fathers had in mind when they created our great nation and its system of government so I could then determine whether *"We the People"* of today's America were holding true to the principles that our founders set forth at the beginning of our journey as a nation. Only by truly understanding our founders' intent can we really know whether we are honoring the tremendous sacrifices they made for us. I fear we have disappointed our founders; and it is my sincere and fervent hope that *"We the People"* will return to the ideals, principles, and beliefs which the founding fathers held true to and which have so nobly advanced the cause of mankind throughout the world over these past two-plus centuries.

I desire also to dedicate this book to four specific individuals, each of whom has had a significant impact on my life and who as a consequence have influenced this work in a great many varied and meaningful ways. These men are all from the small town of Warren, Indiana: George K. Huffman, Russell E. Gilmer, J. Ben Good, and Gordon Laymon. I consider all of these gentlemen to be valued mentors in my life, and I am deeply indebted to their witness and to the legacies of each of their lives in the service of America. These men were of the caliber that Tom Brokaw described in his book *The Greatest Generation*. They each served our nation during time of war, came home, went to work, and seldom ever mentioned it again. In the pages that follow, you will read stories that will help you better appreciate why these men are mentioned.

CONTENTS

FOREWORD

Signing of the Constitution of the United States in 1787: Painting by Howard Chandler Christy

The thirty-nine individuals shown above at the signing of the U.S. Constitution in 1787 had risked their lives, their fortunes, and their sacred honor in order to create a great nation. They then entrusted the preservation and protection of that nation to *"We the People."* Since we are charged with such a huge responsibility, it only stands to reason that we should be required from time to time to step back and consider how we are doing in carrying out our responsibilities. The purpose of this book is to force each of us to ask ourselves whether we are living up to the responsibilities that were given to us by our founders. The United States of America is the oldest surviving constitutional republic made up of a federation of states to ever have been formed. When you reflect upon the fact that the United States comprises just 5 percent of the population and geographic land area of the *entire world* yet it has created more new wealth than all the rest of the world *combined*, one is forced to admit that our founding fathers were on to something when they created this nation!

> *"Are we being true to those people who sacrificed all to give birth to this great democratic experiment?"*

It is essential that *"We the People"* of the United States ask ourselves from time to time, "are we being true to those people who sacrificed all to give birth to this great democratic experiment?" In the pages of this book, you will be shocked to learn that not only have we failed to preserve and protect the nation that has been entrusted to us, but that *"We the People"* have actually allowed it to be substantially *changed* from the intent of our founding fathers. We have allowed our nation, and therefore the principles of our founders, to be abused and corrupted; and this abuse and corruption has, most recently, been accelerating out of control.

> *"America's real challenge of today is not financial. America's real current challenge is that its very survival is at risk."*

The past few years, particularly since late 2008, have been especially difficult ones for America. America is on hard times, but not for the reason that might first come to mind. Yes, our nation has been experiencing some challenges in the stock, bond, and real estate markets due to the fact that we are currently digesting some past financial excesses. But we have gone through these experiences many times in our history. What most people don't understand is that America's real challenge of today is *not* financial. America's *real* current challenge is that its very survival is at risk.

> *America is changing and changing very quickly. No one should necessarily be an alarmist, yet we should all be realists."*

Please understand and be aware that America is changing and changing very quickly. No one should necessarily be an alarmist, yet we should all be realists. We need to examine very closely what is currently transpiring in our government. *"We the People"* have a solemn duty under our Constitution to watch over those to whom we entrust our nation. This book is about America. This book is about our responsibilities as citizens to preserve, protect, and defend America from enemies both foreign and domestic. This book is written with a few simple goals in mind. Those goals are to inspire, educate, and motivate the reader to *thought* and to *action*. America remains the same nation today as at her founding: *the last best hope for man on earth.* We dare not take this for granted, yet I fear that far too many of us have done just that.

Read this book. Consider where you believe America stands today relative to when she was founded. Consider where America is headed. Consider carefully whether *you* should become more involved. It is important to constantly bear in mind what one of our nation's founders and her second president, John Adams, told us at the time of our nation's founding: *"A Constitution of Government once changed from Freedom can never be restored. Liberty, once lost, is lost forever."*

On July 4, 1776, British subjects in the American colonies made it official. On that day, their representatives signed the Declaration of Independence. These Americans made a courageous yet thoughtful and calculated decision to strike out on their own. The colonists chose to no longer be tethered to a government that they deemed to be ruled by tyrants in a faraway place who they determined had lost touch with the colonists' needs and their way of life. It was guaranteed to be a high-risk journey fraught with many uncertainties and huge dangers, and to be a journey that would very likely result in death to many of them. If all of that weren't bad enough, a great majority of the American colonists felt that the gamble they were about to undertake had very little chance of being successful. Yet despite what appeared to be insurmountable odds, these American colonists, fortified by the courage of their convictions and under the leadership of very brave people, decided the risks were worth taking.

These Americans had reached a point at which their patience was totally exhausted. They had given up any hope of positive change, and the circumstances of their day-to-day life under the rule of the British Crown had become intolerable to them. Worse yet, they saw no relief in sight. In their minds, they were being smothered by a government in a faraway place that was operated by people who were making decisions that they deemed counter to what was in their best interests. The British government was constantly imposing taxes and fees on the American colonists to pay for programs that the colonists believed were of absolutely no benefit to them. The colonists also knew that if they didn't act, and act boldly, their children and grandchildren would meet the same intolerable fate. The very thought that *all future* generations would suffer the same burdens of paying for government programs that were against their principles and way of life was more than the American colonists could bear. They felt they had no choice but to act.

Is any of this beginning to sound familiar to *you*? Does any of the above resonate with you given what has been transpiring in America most recently, especially since late 2008 up to and including the present year of 2012?

Deep down, these American people of the eighteenth century knew there had to be a better way to live, a better way to be governed. Their discomfort led them to strike out on what was to become the first American Revolution. With nothing more than the strength of their convictions, they pledged to each other their lives, their fortunes, and their sacred honor, and they struck out on a very long and very uncertain fight for their Freedom and Independence.

This fight would last some eight long years (1775–1783). Just as many of the American colonists had feared, their struggle at various points along the way came very close to meeting with failure and defeat. Yet despite the extreme odds against them, they prevailed. These brave souls won their Freedom. They had defeated the greatest military power on the face of the earth with seemingly nothing more than their own *sheer force of will* and their own *desire for Freedom, Liberty, and a better life*. Their success was nothing short of a miracle.

HISTORY REPEATS ITSELF

Fast-forward nearly two and a half centuries, and you will see the patience of these "same" American people once again being frustrated to the breaking point by a government that many Americans consider to be in a faraway place. Washington DC may not be in a faraway place geographically; however, it is *very* "faraway" as it relates to where the hearts and minds of a great majority of the American people rest today. The American government of the twenty-first century has very clearly lost touch with the needs, desires, hopes, and aspirations of the American people. The American government of today is passing laws and imposing taxes on its citizens to pay for constant new waves of government spending for programs that many of these Americans consider to be foolish boondoggles. It is a government that in just a recent six-month period alone spent not millions, not billions, but quite literally *trillions* of dollars on programs and policies not only that these current Americans feel go against what is in their best interests, but that are in many cases actually at direct variance with and counter to the Constitution that their brave forefathers laid down their lives for more than two centuries earlier.

> *"just as in the 1770s, there are rumblings afoot of ... a second American Revolution."*

The American people in this new twenty-first century are really no different from their forefathers of the late eighteenth century. Just like their forefathers, they know that there most certainly must be a better way to live, a better way to be governed. Just as was the case more than two centuries before, there are once again protests in the streets. Tea parties are being held around the nation in this new century that are eerily similar to and in fact are specifically meant to represent those held by the American colonists in Boston, Massachusetts, just prior to the first American Revolution. Yes, just as in the 1770s, there are rumblings afoot of what could be and, in my view, should be the beginnings of a second American Revolution. Remarkably, this second American Revolution can be easily won. The outcome hinges entirely upon the actions of *today's* American citizens. Details will follow in the pages of this book.

Just what constitutes grounds for revolution by the people against their government? Thomas Jefferson, in the second paragraph of the Declaration of Independence, gives us a very precise answer. While the other founders made multiple changes to much of Jefferson's original Declaration of Independence, they left this part essentially unchanged from the very words chosen by Jefferson. Thomas Jefferson, in America's Declaration of Independence, had this to say on the matter:

> *Governments are instituted among Men, deriving their just powers from the Consent of the Governed, that whenever any Form of Government become destructive to these Ends, it is the Right of the People to alter or to abolish it, and to institute new Government, laying its Foundation on such Principles, and organizing its Powers in such Form, as to them shall seem most likely to effect their Safety and Happiness. Prudence, indeed, will dictate that Governments long established should not be changed for light and transient Causes; and accordingly all Experience hath shewn, that Mankind are more disposed to suffer,*

while Evils are sufferable, than to right themselves by abolishing the Forms to which they are accustomed. But when a long Train of Abuses and Usurpations, pursuing invariably the same Object, evinces a Design to reduce them under absolute Despotism, it is their Right, it is their Duty, to throw off such Government, and to provide new Guards for their future security. Such has been the patient sufferance of these Colonies; and such is now the necessity which constrains them to alter their former Systems of Government...."

So there you have it. Governments are created and instituted by people and get their powers from the consent of the governed. If government becomes destructive to the ends for which it was established, it is *the right,* it is *the duty,* of the people to alter or abolish *that* government and to institute a *new* government. Were Jefferson to have stopped there, one could argue in favor of revolution at most any turn or change of events. But he didn't stop there. Jefferson was careful to provide what we shall describe as a "qualifying statement". Jefferson explained experience has shown that men should suffer as much evil as they can withstand, over as long a period as possible, and not dissolve government for "light and transient" reasons. Jefferson went on to say that, in fact, experience has shown that people are *likely* to suffer for long periods rather than to overturn, alter, or abolish their government. Here, Jefferson is arguing that "patience is a virtue." After these very careful words of caution, Jefferson clearly stated that if the government, after a long series of "abuses and usurpations," has designed and pursued the destructive end to the people's life, Liberty, and pursuit of happiness, that it is not just their right, "it is their duty," to overturn, alter, or abolish such government.

"a significant altering of our government ... is actually the only means of saving it."

I believe **"We the People"** have arrived at such a place *in our time* within the United States of America. In this book, you will find the evidence with which I intend to prove this claim. Please bear in mind that I *do not* call for overturning or abolishing the government of the United States. However, I *do call* for a significant *altering* of our government, and in fact argue this significant altering of our government is actually the only means of saving our Republic from what will otherwise be its certain destruction and demise.

*"**We the People***' *have been suffering a 'long train of abuses and usurpations' by our government ... "*

We have been without a real American Revolution since 1776. That is 236 years. Based on the history of most governments, we are long overdue for a change. In many respects, it is something of a miracle that we have survived this long without one. While I would like it to be otherwise, "**We the People**" have been suffering a "long train of abuses and usurpations" by our government, and our leaders are threatening the very future of our great Republic. Our government, most recently in their takeover of much of the banking, insurance, and auto industries, has ignored long-held property rights and ignored the very rule of law. While it appeared for a brief moment that the U.S. Supreme Court would intervene with some sanity, in the end they themselves rolled over and failed to do the right thing. Our government has piled up so much debt on the backs of future generations of Americans that we will have little choice but to default on our empty promises. Chinese and other foreigners hold some *$3 trillion* of our debt and laugh in the face of our "promise to pay." "**We the People**" must act *now* in order to restore any hope of future credibility.

> *"**God forbid we should ever be twenty years without such a rebellion. The people cannot be all, and always, well informed. The part which is wrong will be discontented, in proportion to the importance of the facts they misconceive. If they remain quiet under such misconceptions, it is lethargy, the forerunner of death to the public liberty ... What country before ever existed a century and half without a rebellion? And what country can preserve its liberties if their rulers are not warned from time to time that their people preserve the spirit of resistance? Let them take arms. The remedy is to set them right as to facts, pardon and pacify them. What signify a few lives lost in a century or two? The tree of liberty must be refreshed from time to time with the blood of patriots and tyrants. It is its natural manure."***
>
> —**Thomas Jefferson**, in a letter to William Stephens Smith, November 13, 1787, referring to Shays' Rebellion

"I hold it, that a little rebellion, now and then, is a good thing, and as necessary in the political world as storms in the physical."

—**Thomas Jefferson**, in a letter to James Madison, January 30, 1787, referring to Shays' Rebellion

Thomas Jefferson

Author of America's Declaration of Independence and third U.S. President
Born April 13, 1743 – Died July 4, 1826

INTRODUCTION

hy this book? Why now? Believe it or not, this is an "accidental" book. It came about in response to requests from others to finish what this farmer from Indiana had started in an e-mail to Glenn Beck (a prominent radio and television personality at the time this is being written) in March 2009. That e-mail was a sort of "rant" that your author wrote Glenn in response to a particular law that the U.S. Congress had just passed. March 2009 was when the U.S. House of Representatives passed a law that would tax a "specific class" of U.S. citizens on their income at a rate of 90 percent. Surprisingly, what really brought out the anger that led to the rant was *not* the 90 percent tax rate, although that would have been reason enough to be furious. What angered me more than the 90 percent tax rate was the sheer unbridled arrogance and hypocrisy that our so-called representatives in Congress demonstrated in passing this law.

The entire episode centered on certain bonuses that had been paid to employees of an American company, American International Group (AIG). The irony of this whole episode was that the people (the U.S. Congress) who now were determined to take the bonuses away had actually been the very people who had granted the bonuses to this "specific class" of U.S. citizens in the first place! Many have argued that what the U.S. House members did was unconstitutional, for they cite that singling out and taxing a "specific class" of people is prohibited in the U.S. Constitution. Either way, passing this law was perfect proof that these so-called representatives of the people in Congress were either extremely arrogant or stupid, or worse yet, both. As far as I was concerned, it didn't really matter whether members of Congress were arrogant or simply stupid. What really mattered was that something had to be done, and this farmer from Indiana could no longer in good conscience remain silent. Thus was born the following e-mail rant to Glenn Beck.

> *"you cannot repair damages done from unwise lending practices by attempting to "paper over" the problem with excessive government borrowing and spending."*

Dear Glenn,

*Thank you for being the voice for a great many Americans. I am a farmer from Indiana. I was raised on a farm near a small town in the American Midwest. I spent ten years attending college on a part-time basis while simultaneously working full-time as a self-employed independent insurance agent and real estate broker. I was a great admirer and a huge supporter of Ronald Reagan. For the past thirty years during my adult life and working years, I have continued to be self-employed and live on the farm. To say that I am fed up with our elected officials would be an understatement. Like many Americans, I have actually been frustrated for years watching our elected leaders quite literally "sell our country down the river" while lining their own pockets and at the same time doing all they can to insulate themselves from any sort of accountability for their actions. What infuriates a farmer from Indiana more than the money they waste while recklessly bankrupting our nation is the outright unbridled arrogance they seem to flaunt while doing it. When the financial mortgage crisis began to unfold last September, our elected officials did what this farmer and many other people consider to be exactly the wrong thing. Instead of allowing the financial excesses to "naturally wring themselves out" of our economic system, our elected so-called representatives seized the moment to intervene with an insane fix that will most likely only serve to make matters much worse. Simple logic dictates that you cannot repair damages done from unwise lending practices by attempting to "paper over" the problem with excessive government borrowing and spending. This is lunacy, it is un-American, and it must come to an end. If we continue this behavior, the very existence of our great Republic is at serious risk. "**We the People**" are flirting with disaster.*

> *"There is no practice more dangerous than that of borrowing money."*
> —**George Washington,** July 12, 1797

I was fortunate to serve on the board of a local community bank for many years. If I were to cite the most important fundamental principle that I learned during that experience, it would be that you cannot fix mistakes in borrowing and lending by throwing good money after bad. It's akin to trying to cure an alcoholic with another bottle of Wild Turkey; however, this is precisely the approach that our government has been taking recently in attempting to "bail out" our banking and insurance industries. The behavior of our government over the past six months has put this farmer from Indiana over the edge. Our founders by now have to be literally rolling over in their graves. Glenn, the time has now arrived for a ***"Second American Revolution."***

OUR 2ND AMERICAN REVOLUTION

> *"we must once again begin to follow the Constitution that our founders so courageously fought and died for … we must dismantle much of the current federal government and dramatically reduce its size."*

What do I mean by a second American Revolution? I mean that we must take our government back from the elitist, career politicians who have bankrupted our nation by virtue of allowing themselves to be manipulated, bought, sold, and corrupted by many and varied greedy special interest groups. Quite simply, I mean that we must once again begin to follow the Constitution that our founders so courageously fought and died for and so wisely created for us. In very simple terms, I mean that we must dismantle much of the current federal government and dramatically reduce its size.

Our founders, through the Constitution, called for the federal government's role in Americans' lives to be almost nonexistent. Essentially the only roles the federal government was to have in the affairs of the people were to provide for the defense of the nation, issue and coin money, handle foreign affairs, and regulate interstate commerce. In other words, the federal government was only to have power over and take care of those very few items that the people and the states could not accomplish for themselves. The founders were very adamant about severely limiting the role of our central government. In fact, in our Constitution, the founders actually spoke more about what a central government was not allowed to do than they did about what it was allowed to do. They intended for the American people to live their lives free of any governmental interference. If there were to be decisions made by government, our founders desired that those decisions be made at the very lowest level by local and state governments. The founders of our nation also clearly understood that decisions affecting the everyday lives of people are best made by the specific people that those decisions will impact, primarily the people's families and most certainly not any form of government.

For the majority of our founding fathers, government was considered really nothing more or less than a necessary evil. Thomas Paine, the man who authored the famous pamphlet Common Sense, written in January 1776, evidences our founding fathers' intent best in the following statement:

> "Society in every state is a blessing, but government, even in its best state, is but a necessary evil; in its worst state, an intolerable one."
>
> —**Thomas Paine,** Common Sense, 1776

These brilliant men understood that there must be accountability for decisions made by elected officials. They also understood that accountability can really only best be provided on a very local, face-to-face level. They wrote our Constitution to accomplish this by specifically limiting national government, leaving the bulk of the power in the States. Isn't it amazing how smart these guys were? Actually, we should not be surprised or amazed by their superior intellect, for these were exceptionally learned men. Even so, given the magnitude of what they were able to accomplish, divine providence was very likely at work in and through these people.

WHAT MUST TAKE PLACE

Just what must occur, and how will this second American Revolution take place? First and foremost, we must now do what Newt Gingrich and others in Congress tried but failed to accomplish in the "Contract with America" in 1994. **"We the People"** must insist on having an amendment to the U.S. Constitution that mandates term limits for our elected federal representatives. With 80 percent of the American people in favor of term limits, the debate should not be whether we will have them, but rather what form they should take. My idea is that the U.S. House should be limited to four terms and that the U.S. Senate should be limited to two terms. This would equate to a maximum of eight years for the House and twelve years for the Senate. We may want to change the House terms to four years. This would allow elected officials more time to get things done and not exhaust the representatives and the electorate with nonstop election cycles. In any event, no one person should be allowed to serve longer than twelve years in a federal office. In addition, elected leaders should not be allowed to run for a new office while they are serving in their current one. Once an elected leader has served two terms in one office, they should not be allowed to run for any other office; the only exception being if we have a real statesman on our hands and that person desires to compete for the presidency.

> *"We need to return to those days of Lincoln when we had 'citizen' statesmen."*

Term limits will keep ideas fresh by involving more folks. Once in place, we will again enjoy the benefits of a true "representative" government. Oh yes, by the way, since there will no longer be career jobs for elected officials, **"We the People"** will no longer provide special pensions for elected officials, nor special health care benefits, nor private gyms and barber shops, no special treatment of any kind. The only compensation will be a stipend or nominal "living wage," just like we had at our founding and up through Abraham Lincoln's day. Lincoln ran for the U.S. House of Representatives in 1846, and he won a two-year term. At that time there was an understanding that, when elected, you served one term and went home and back to work in the "real world." Despite the fact that Lincoln loved the job and would probably have been reelected, he honored the tradition and did not seek a second term. We need to return to those days of Lincoln when we had "citizen" statesmen. In our new and improved system, we will once again have elected officials who are not in it for the money and power but rather to simply serve their country. And let's face it, once we get finished dismantling much of the federal government, there will not be that much for these people to do. Oh yes, one other thing, elected officials will now govern from their home districts. With today's modern computer technology, meetings can be held via teleconference literally from the official's "home office." All of their telephone calls and teleconferences will be held on an "open line." That way, any American can dial in and "listen in" at will. This will result in total transparency and will make it easier for our public servants to avoid corruption. Washington DC will pretty much become a "museum" where the president lives and where Congress meets a few times each year.

> *"We are going to revert back to the system that our founders originally created for us and that they outlined so eloquently for us in our United States Constitution."*

Second, we must dismantle much of the U.S. federal government. While this dismantling will take some time to complete, the final result will be more than worth the effort. Within a short time, over half of what the federal government now "attempts" to do for the people will be done much more efficiently and effectively on a local level by families, churches, and neighborhoods or by local and state governments. The result will be that we will once again have the Federalism that our founders gave us originally and that Ronald Reagan so wisely reminded us that we needed to restore. Social Security will "over time" gradually be privatized. Federal programs such as Medicare, Medicaid, welfare, unemployment (and the list goes on and on ad infinitum) will cease to exist on a federal level. Family, friends, neighbors, churches, and local governments will provide these services for people on an entirely local level, where accountability will once again be possible. There are many details to be worked out, but you get the idea. We are going to revert back to the system that our founders originally created for us and that they outlined so eloquently for us in our United States Constitution. This system worked exceedingly well for us during the course of more than the first half of our existence as a nation, and there is no reason to believe that it won't work again.

*Critics will say that this approach won't work, that this is a "different time." They will argue that the American people of today won't care for their own, that they won't pick up where the government leaves off. They will say that society will break down, that anarchy will result. I completely and totally reject this premise. To the contrary, I have a deep and abiding faith in the American people. If **"We the People"** simply get the federal government out of the way of the people, we will unleash "the miracle that is America." The ideals and principles that our founders used in creating our great nation are unchanging and timeless. These same ideals and principles will work just as well in our current time as they did more than two centuries ago during their time.*

*Third, we must honor our obligations. That begs the following question: What are we going to do about the now-more-than $15 trillion of debt that our politicians have created while corrupting our system and wasting our money? That's real simple—we will pay it off. There's a new and novel idea for you. Something dawned on me while I was driving down the California coast one day this past winter. As I drove for miles and miles along the Pacific Ocean enjoying the sunset, I couldn't help but notice that there was nothing anywhere to be seen. By this I mean there were no buildings, no roads, no people, nothing. This was not particularly unusual because I was driving through a military base. The federal government owns some of the most desirable and valuable real estate in the United States; and they own LOTS of it! Whatever **"We the People"** are doing on this prime real estate (with the exception of Navy bases) can just as easily be accomplished on some of the ugliest real estate in the United States, which the federal government also owns—areas like the Arizona and Nevada deserts. So no* *problem; we will simply move these functions to the less desirable ugly real estate and sell off the extremely valuable prime real estate to private developers and use those funds to help pay off the national debt.*

> *"It will actually be a very enjoyable and liberating experience dismantling the federal government."*

*Keep in mind that selling valuable, prime real estate is just one idea. Once the process begins, **"We the People"** will be able to come up with endless lists of excellent ways to save money, raise funds, sell off government assets, completely eliminate government programs, etc. It will actually be a very enjoyable and liberating experience dismantling the federal government. This process will be much like private sector bankruptcy reorganization, only on a national scale. If there's money left over when we are finished, we can create a federal surplus to be used for future defense needs or we can hand the excess money over to the states on a per capita basis to pay for the unfunded Social Security and Medicare liabilities that they are going to have to figure out how to cover. While we are at it, we will also by now have put in place a federal balanced budget amendment and a presidential line item veto for the budget process to protect ourselves from ever again having to suffer from this sort of insanity in our future.*

You may have noticed that I have been picking on the Congress. Not to worry, similar restrictions will be placed on the presidency. The presidency will take on a much more conservative and modest air. Just as in the case of the Congress, much of what the president has been occupied with will no longer be required. Since most of what both branches of Congress have been doing will be returned to the states, eliminated, or privatized, much of our bloated federal bureaucracy will likewise no longer be necessary and will cease to exist. Just think, no longer will the president spend a cool million dollars of taxpayer money flying Air Force One back and forth to Denver or Phoenix simply to celebrate spending $787 billion on a stupid and needless stimulus package full of pork projects that shouldn't have been passed in the first place! In this new environment of back-to-basics government, such folly will not even cross the president's mind. Won't that be great?

> *The course we are now on will most certainly result in some form of a second American Revolution."*

Fourth, we must revert back to the days when we actually followed the U.S. Constitution. We owe this not just to the rule of law but also to the honor and the sacrifices of our founders. The founders of our Republic were willing to make enormous personal sacrifices in creating this nation of ours. We have disrespected them tremendously by our actions. What is equally important is that our actions also dishonor the sacrifice made by the generations who have come before us, our forefathers, who died on the battlefield and who gave of themselves so selflessly. This current insane behavior by our federal government is unsustainable and will come to an end very soon one way or another.

Our founders wisely warned us that if the American people were not vigilant, the consequences that **"We the People"** *are now experiencing would at some point occur in our future. We should not be surprised these brilliant men would be correct in their predictions. Many will say that this dream of a second American Revolution occurring on a peaceful basis, as outlined above, is simply a pipe dream. Perhaps they are correct. Only time will tell. There is one thing that is certain. The course we are now on will most certainly result in some form of a second American Revolution. Let us hope and pray that we can shepherd our great nation through it peacefully and with honor.*

—William E. Shuttleworth, Warren, IN

I didn't really expect that Glenn Beck would respond to this e-mail, and Glenn didn't disappoint me. However, at the same moment I sent the e-mail to Glenn, I also sent it to several friends and acquaintances. The e-mail struck a nerve with many of these folks. They forwarded it to several additional people. Before long I was hearing from people all over America who had read the e-mail and wanted to hear more. You see, these people, along with literally millions of other hardworking Americans, were also fed up with what had been transpiring. Many of these folks were now encouraging me to write more on the subject and to make a project of the issue. It led to a great deal of research, and that is how this "accidental book" was born.

"our founding fathers … are the "real" authors."

I had never authored a book before, and I had no earthly idea that there was a book "in me." However, I did have a sincere desire to do what I could to help save our great nation and was thereby motivated to make the effort. All that was left to do was to write the book. Less than a year later, this book was born. A "ghostwriter" did not write this book. I wrote every word of it, except the most important and powerful words, those being the words of our founding fathers. They are the "real" authors. Absent the founders' words, the effort would not have been necessary. It was for them that this work was undertaken. I hope that you enjoy the book. More importantly, I sincerely hope that you will embark on this journey with me to save our Republic.

*"your author recommends … "A Nine (9) Point Plan to
Save America from an otherwise Certain Demise"*

Before you begin reading Chapter 1, I recommend you go to Chapter 10 at the end of this book and read *"A Nine (9) Point Plan to Save America from an otherwise Certain Demise,"* as this is the "heart and soul" of <u>Our 2nd American Revolution</u>. Reviewing these nine (9) goals *first* will provide you an excellent "primer" and outline. This information will most certainly be of help to you in better understanding the intent and thesis of the entire book.

You will find included in this book, in their original form and spelling, the Declaration of Independence and the Constitution of the United States. These documents are there for your active review and reference. The strength of these documents lies in their brevity. These documents form the entire basis for our nation's existence. Yet both documents *combined* are only twenty-seven pages in length, compared to the $787 billion economic stimulus bill of March 2009 at over 1,000 pages or the IRS income tax code, which comprises more than 66,000 pages. We all have much to learn from our founders in many areas. Perhaps we should start with their lesson of being succinct. These documents have been placed at the very "center" of the book, between Chapters 5 and 6, rather than at the end of the book, as is often customary. Their placement in the center of the book is by design, to remind us that **"We the People"** need to keep these documents "at the very center" of all we say and do as we go about conducting the business of our great nation. Let us now begin with Chapter 1.

CHAPTER ONE

SETTING SOME GROUND RULES FOR THIS BOOK

I t is important that we clear the air about something from the outset. This is not meant to be a "political" book. By that, I mean these writings are not intended to promote one political party or political philosophy over any other. I have no "axe to grind" with *any* political figure or *any* political party. This book is simply about what is best for *America*. In the interest of full disclosure, and as you read in the email to Glenn Beck that appeared in the introduction, I was a great admirer and an unapologetic supporter of Ronald Reagan. From that, you might have concluded that I consider myself to be a member of the Republican Party. You may have further concluded that this would be a book with a goal of convincing you to embrace the philosophy of the Republican Party. If those were your conclusions or assumptions, you have been wrong. Please understand: during the Reagan era, I did indeed consider myself to be a Republican. Now, however, I feel as though I am a man without a party. Ronald Reagan pointed out in his explanation of why he had changed from a Democrat to a Republican that he hadn't left the Democratic Party, it had left him. I have that same sensation today. I have not left the Republican Party; the Republican Party has left me. I am therefore currently a man without a party.

As I see it, when measured against what our founders had in mind for us, there is not one whit of difference between the two major political parties in this country. They have both lost their way. For my purposes, they may as well consider themselves as one party under the name of either the "Dempublicans" or "Republicrats." While I am especially shocked as well as fed up with the actions taken by Barack Obama since he became president, you should also know that I have been equally or perhaps even more angry with the actions taken by George W. Bush and the Republicans. We could have expected what we have gotten from Barack Obama.

1

> *"George W. Bush governed at a time when he could have made a real difference for this nation, but he failed to 'seize the moment.'"*

But George W. Bush was disingenuous. George W. Bush and the Republicans claimed to be conservative, yet they governed as socialists. George W. Bush's presidency was, as this farmer from Indiana sees it, a very big lost opportunity. George W. Bush governed at a time when he could have made a real difference for this nation, but he failed to "seize the moment." He could have vetoed spending, but he didn't. He could have taken steps to protect our borders and stop illegal immigration, but he didn't. He could have focused on the real war on terror by exclusively hunting down and killing Osama bin Laden and Al-Qaeda, but he didn't. He could have let the mortgage crisis run its natural course, but he didn't. George Bush did keep us safe after 9/11, and for that we can all be grateful. But make no mistake: I am just as disappointed and angered with George W. Bush and the Republicans' behavior as I am with the behavior of Barack Obama and our so-called representatives in Congress. We have big problems to solve. These are *not* the people to solve them.

"TEA PARTY"

For all of the reasons stated above, I now consider myself to be a member of the "Tea Party." You most certainly have heard of the Tea Party movement taking place all across America in 2009 and 2010. But you are probably saying, *"I didn't know that there was actually an organized political party called the Tea Party."* That's because there isn't. It doesn't exist—yet. Do you realize that there are more than a hundred political parties in the United States? It seems that there is a political party for every splinter group you can put a name to. Unfortunately, there is not one political party, with the possible exception of the Constitution Party, which truly focuses on and makes every effort to follow the U.S. Constitution and the principles, tenets, and beliefs of our nation's founders—that is, until now. With more than one hundred political parties already in existence in the United States, you might be asking, *"why create one more?"* We need to create a new one for the simple reason that none of our current political parties stand for redeeming our great nation from the error of our past and present ways. I see it as the only way to right our wrongs.

We must be bold. We have evolved to where we are today slowly and incrementally, over a period of mostly the past seventy to eighty years. However, the only way for us to bring our nation back to the roots of our founders will be to make some very dramatic and bold moves. There are simply too many firmly entrenched special interest groups in place for us to accomplish it in any other manner. Besides, the people currently in power in the Democrat and Republican parties will not give up easily. Our elitist, career politicians firmly believe they are just the people needed to solve our nation's problems. These people think that even larger government and, more specifically, the new government programs that *they* create are just the prescription that will cure our nation's ills. There are also millions of well-meaning people who steadfastly believe, despite all of the clear and consistent overwhelming past evidence proving they are dead wrong, that more and bigger government is the answer. The actions of our elected leaders have been insane, for as we all know, insanity is doing the same thing over and over again and expecting a different result. Our current elected officials and their contemporaries will not go away quietly.

> *"This second American Revolution will not be about 'tinkering at the margins or nibbling at the edges' of our national problems. Fighting a revolution requires not caretakers, but people who **really care**."*

What this country needs is a grassroots movement under strong new leadership with a very bold new agenda of major reforms in government, beginning with the passage of a Term Limits Amendment to the Constitution for our elected and appointed federal officials, significant reductions in government programs and spending, a Balanced Budget, and a Presidential Line Item Veto Amendment, as well as many other reforms that you will read about in this book. This second American Revolution will not be about "tinkering at the margins or nibbling at the edges" of our national problems. Our past few decades of mismanagement require that we make wholesale changes in how our government operates and functions. It is simply not realistic to expect that any of our current incumbent politicians have the wisdom or the courage to make good decisions for our nation going forward. They have been entirely derelict in their duties, and their services are therefore no longer needed. What the United States now needs is a new approach to governance under the leadership of a new set of commonsense "citizen" statesmen. We need people who are motivated solely by what is in the best interest of the future of our great nation. There is only one means of fighting a successful revolution, and that is with revolutionaries. Fighting a revolution requires not caretakers, but people who *really care.*

Now all of that being said, and to be totally fair, I would not rule out the possibility that our two major political parties might put forward candidates who are real reformers. But take note that these folks come from the states, not the federal government. I have serious doubts about the two parties' ability to fill the roles needed from their current ranks and most particularly those already in office. The big money and special interests are simply too well entrenched within these establishments to allow the two major parties to stray very far away from the status quo—and don't forget, it's the status quo that is *killing* America. This revolution, like every successful revolution, will require true revolutionaries to fight and to win it. That is why I am suggesting that we need a new political party. What more fitting name could it have than the "Tea Party"?

> *"While I in no way feel that I have left America, in a great many ways, I feel that America has left me ... Our elected leaders have slowly and insidiously moved away from following our Constitution."*

I mentioned earlier that I consider myself to be a man without a party. In a great many ways, I feel as though I am a man without a country and actually often think of myself as a man living in a foreign land. Hearing me say that I feel like a man without a country or living in a foreign land may sound extreme to you. I hope that it does. It is intended as such. While I in no way feel that I have left America, in a great many ways, I feel that America has left me. Neither of the two major political parties truly supports the fundamental principles of our nation's founders, yet they are running our nation. It is for this reason that I say in many respects I consider myself to be a man living in a foreign land. Our elected leaders have slowly and insidiously moved away from following our Constitution. As a result, America is not the same country that I grew up in and learned to love and appreciate so much as a child and young adult. It deeply saddens me to witness that *"We the People"* have allowed America to drift so far away from the principles that in our early beginnings made us the greatest nation on the face of the earth. I am totally confident that if George Washington, Thomas Jefferson, John Adams, and Ronald Reagan were living today, they would share these same sentiments. I know that millions of Americans are also deeply concerned about these matters.

"A little matter will move a party, but it must be something great that moves a nation."

—**Thomas Paine,** *Rights of Man*, 1792
Born in England in 1737 – Died in America in 1809

"The cause of America is, in a great measure, the cause of all mankind."

—**Thomas Paine,** *Common Sense*, 1776

What You Can Expect from This Book

There has been much said lately by many different individuals and groups on the subject of the government's activist intervention in our economy and in the individual daily lives of our people. There has been no shortage of yelling, screaming, complaining, and gnashing of teeth by politicians and the talking heads on television about what the government has been doing or not doing. However, what has been glaringly absent from all of this noise have been any meaningful, specific, concrete ideas or suggestions on what *should* have been done in contrast to what *has* or *has not* been done. As a result, in my view, *all* of these people have been quite simply wasting their time. These people have only been "tinkering at the margins and nibbling at the edges" of the real central problems that confront our nation. What you will find in this book are the author's observations of where we have gone wrong as a nation, but only as filtered through the eyes of our founding fathers.

> *"The problems that we face in our nation are enormous, and they will require bold measures as well as thinking and approaches to problem solving that are "outside the box" of conventional reasoning."*

More importantly, however, you will also find at the end of each chapter specific suggestions and specific recommendations on solutions designed to *fix* the many problems that confront America. Please understand that I am under no illusion that you will agree with everything that I have to say; however, I can guarantee that you will "enjoy the read." Many of the comments, suggestions, and ideas in this book you will very likely *not* have heard before now. Many of the solutions that will be offered in this book you might believe to be unconventional or even impractical. That is okay. The problems that we face in our nation are enormous, and they will require bold measures as well as thinking and approaches to problem solving that are "outside the box" of conventional reasoning. My primary goal in writing this book is to simply get people to *think* and *act*. When you are finished reading this book, you will clearly understand where this farmer from Indiana stands on solving our nation's problems. It is also my sincere desire that you will have a much better appreciation of how awesome and thoughtful our founders and forefathers were. What is being proposed involves some very *fundamental* changes to our current political system as well as to our very system of government. For this reason, much of what is proposed will be viewed by many of you as radical, impossible to achieve, or both.

> *"all of the changes that are proposed in this book are based upon what our founders and forefathers had to say on the matter."*

That said, please bear in mind that *all* of the changes that are proposed in this book are based upon what our founders and forefathers had to say on the matter. In this book, you will be hearing *directly* from the founders of this great nation, from many of our wise forefathers (like Abraham Lincoln), from many of the other great minds from our nation's past, and from some of our current leaders who are still alive and doing well today. If you are like millions of other Americans, you are very likely extremely frustrated with the direction in which our nation is headed. You realize America is on the wrong track, but you are at a loss as to what to do or how to help bring her back. This book will provide you great relief. Don't worry; you will not be required to run for office. All that is required of you in order to play a critical role in bringing America back from the brink of otherwise certain destruction and demise is to go to the polls and *vote*. It is really just that simple! Vote, and you will be a soldier in the silent revolution to take back America. If enough of us exercise our right to vote, on that very day we will begin to release America from her bondage to debt and misery and put her back on track for a brilliant future. While reading this book will be a sad and sobering experience due to the truth telling about how we have allowed America to fail her founders and our heritage, it will also be a joyful experience due to our discussion of the real *possibilities* we have for correcting the error of our ways and rebuilding America back to her former glory. It *can* be done.

Here Is Just One Example of a Proposed Change

> *Oligarchy defined: a small group of people who together govern a nation or control an organization, often for their own purposes.*

> *"we have really accomplished nothing more than to replace a foreign royal monarchy of the eighteenth century with a new domestic royal oligarchy of the twenty-first century."*

One example of what you will find in this book is a proposal that **"We the People"** join together in a grassroots movement to insist that the U.S. Congress vote on and pass an amendment to the U.S. Constitution limiting the terms of our U.S. House Representatives and Senators. I see this as the *only* way to fix our current corrupt political system. My position is that by virtue of allowing politicians to make a career of their positions as elected officials, over time we have really accomplished nothing more than to replace a foreign royal monarchy of the eighteenth century with a new domestic royal oligarchy of the twenty-first century. As a result, most all of our elected officials have lost touch with and are actually totally clueless about what their constituents think, much less what those constituents expect from them. The reality of this is proven every day by what they say and do. Despite this, these elected officials enjoy a 95 percent lock on reelection. This needs to change, and with 80 percent of the nation's population now in favor of term limits, it appears that the time is finally right to bring it to pass.

"in those old days we had a constant flow of fresh ideas and truly representative government."

There was a time when our country was first founded that politicians sought elective office for all of the *right* reasons. They ran to serve their country and to truly represent their constituents at home. They limited their terms *voluntarily.* As a result, we had a healthy democratic Republic due to the fact that in those old days we had a constant flow of fresh ideas and truly representative government. Perhaps the best, and likely the most famous, example of this was the case of Abraham Lincoln. Lincoln was elected to the U.S. Congress in 1846 as a U.S. House Representative from Illinois. He absolutely loved the job and would have preferred to run for reelection in 1848. Setting his personal desires aside, Lincoln stood down and allowed others to run and serve in his district. During that time in our history, it was understood that you served your term and then went home and "back to work in the real world." As a result of this long-held tradition, the United States had a government that was a true representative Republic during the first century and more of her existence.

Unfortunately, during the course of the twentieth century, we have replaced that tradition and have evolved into a career political system with a more than 95 percent reelection rate for incumbents. In the process, we have lost any real semblance of a representative democracy as well as any chance to have a constant flow of fresh ideas "bubbling up from the people," as was the case in the early days of our Republic. The result of this has been an insidious brain drain and a "dummying-down" of our government. The only real solution to fix this problem is to simply make it *illegal* to stay in office as a career. This can easily be accomplished via an amendment to the U.S. Constitution. In addition, we will no longer provide elected leaders fast-vesting lifetime pensions, private dining rooms, cradle-to-grave health care, personal barbershops, private gyms, big staffs, and a list of special treatments too long to print here. More details will follow in this book.

"The happiness of society is the end of government."
—**John Adams**, 1776

"Whenever the people are well informed, they can be trusted with their own government; that whenever things get so far wrong as to attract their notice, they may be relied on to set them to rights."

—**Thomas Jefferson,** in a letter to Richard Price, January 8, 1789

THE UNITED STATES CONSTITUTION

"We the People" have allowed our elected leaders to *abuse* the Constitution. In our early days as a nation, the Constitution was referred to often, and the people required that their elected leaders follow it. Thomas Jefferson felt that the Tenth Amendment within the Bill of Rights, which limits the powers of the national government and reserves all rights that are not specifically granted to the national government within that document to the states and to the people, formed the *very essence* of the document. We have now allowed it to be interpreted *exactly in the reverse* of this intent. The Tenth Amendment was placed there with the express purpose to avoid what the thirteen American colonies were forced to endure under British rule. Our founders specifically intended that any political decisions be made at the very lowest level in society, where *accountability* is possible and government control could be maintained.

"the General Welfare clause says 'promote' the General Welfare, not 'provide' the General Welfare."

Our Constitution, if it is anything, is a document of negatives *limiting* the national government. This fact has frustrated aggressive political leaders since our founding, and it continues to be a great source of frustration to them today. That was *precisely the intent* of our founding fathers. It wasn't that they were trying to be sadistic; they simply valued Freedom and Liberty above all else, and they had the wisdom to know what would happen if these rules were not adhered to. Should not *"We the People"* honor their wishes? By the way, the General Welfare clause says "promote" the General Welfare, not "provide" the General Welfare.

BALLOTS, NOT BULLETS

"This time around, we can and we must use ballots instead of bullets."

Our founding fathers during the first American Revolution were left with but *one* choice. Their fight for Freedom, Liberty, and the change that they desired would of necessity have to be fought and won with bullets, as well as the shedding of their own blood. Fortunately, *"We the People"* of America in the twenty-first century have the luxury of an entirely *different* course of action. *We* are able to redeem our Freedom and Liberty and bring about the change that *"We the People"* desire simply by becoming more engaged and casting ballots in a box. Ours will be a *silent* revolution. Not silent in crying out for and insisting upon a return to the blessings of Liberty and Freedom, but silent in terms of the traditional means of violence and bloodshed that often accompany revolution. *"We the People"* will simply show up in enormous and unprecedented numbers and *vote*. Once again the American people will revolutionize the world. *"We the People"* of the twenty-first century are in this enviable position because of the sacrifices of our founders in the first American Revolution *and* due to their forming our entirely unique system of government under the U.S. Constitution. It is the sincere hope and prayer of this farmer from Indiana that our second American Revolution will be fought and won, not with the shedding of blood, but rather with an active and engaged electorate who are dedicated to honoring the sacrifices made by those who have come before us. This time around, we can *and we must* use ballots instead of bullets.

"WE THE PEOPLE"

"It seems that a great many American citizens living today have forgotten, or perhaps never really fully understood, that our system of government was designed so that the ultimate power in the decision making for our great nation rests with 'We the People.'"

Quite frequently throughout this book, you will see the words *"We the People"* shown in this identical format. This has been done purposely and to provide emphasis. It seems that a great many American citizens living today have forgotten, or perhaps never really fully understood, that our system of government was designed so that the *ultimate power* in the decision making for our great nation rests with *"We the People."* This ignorance on the part of many Americans has not necessarily been the fault "of the people." Instead, it has been due to our collective neglect in teaching these principles to our citizens through good education. It seems that *"We the People"* no longer insist that our youth are taught the fundamentals of how our system of government operates. However, regardless of where our failures rest, we *all* must remember that *"We the People"* are responsible for educating Americans about the *huge* importance of these principles. George Washington reminded us *all* of the *people's power* at our founding in 1787 when he said after the Constitutional Convention:

> *"The power under the Constitution will always be with the people. It is entrusted for certain defined purposes, and for a certain limited period, to representatives of their own choosing; and whenever it is executed contrary to their interest, or not agreeable to their wishes, their servants can, and undoubtedly will, be recalled."*
>
> **—George Washington,** after the Constitutional Convention

> *"... our founders began the U.S. Constitution with: 'We the People'... They simply desired to remind us of our power."*

It was no mistake that our founders began the U.S. Constitution with: *"'We the People' of the United States, in order to form a more perfect union ..."* They simply desired to remind us of *our* power. *"We the People"* is being used throughout this book in this format so that we may *all* learn to better appreciate and be constantly reminded of the glorious gift that God has given us through the actions of our founding fathers. In this way, we may each better appreciate the responsibility that we *all* have to honor that gift.

FREEDOM AND LIBERTY

Throughout this book, you will find the words Freedom and Liberty capitalized. Once again, this is done to provide emphasis. One goal of this book is to stimulate a renewed awareness of and appreciation for what our founders and forefathers gave us when they fought and died for our Freedom and Liberty. Therefore, it only seems fitting and proper that we show these words in capital form when these two principles are referred to within the pages of this book. Besides, at the time of our founding, nouns were very often capitalized when they appeared in written form. You will see the evidence of this later as you read the U.S. Constitution that appears in the center of this book in its original form. I have also included the Declaration of Independence in the same section of this book.

CHAPTER TWO

HOW AMERICA HAS LOST HER WAY

WHAT WENT WRONG?

"We have become a lazy and apathetic people who have gradually, yet willingly, surrendered the greatest gift that God has ever bestowed upon a people."

Just after the Revolutionary War, and continuing for more than a century thereafter, *"We the People"* held true to what our founders had given us. What our founders so thoughtfully provided us was a *true representative Republic.* Then, early in the twentieth century, we began to allow our freedoms to be taken away, and our nation slowly but surely migrated toward a *socialist* state in which we forfeited our rights to control our own individual destiny. Perhaps we did this unwittingly; however, either way, we slowly and surely gave up what Abraham Lincoln so eloquently described as a nation *"of the people, by the people, and for the people."* One issue at a time and one election at a time, we gradually allowed our government to be transformed from a representative Republic to a royal oligarchy governed by a set of elitist, career politicians with a mentality that they know better than the citizen as to what is in that citizen's best interest. We have become a lazy and apathetic people who have gradually, yet willingly, surrendered the greatest gift that God has ever bestowed upon a people—that gift being the Freedom to live our lives unmolested by a tyrannical government. The time is *now* for each of us to wake up and to once again become active in determining the destiny of our great nation. *"We the People"* *must* become engaged. It is time for "Mr.

Smith" to go to Washington; it is time for many of us to become *"citizen"* statesmen.

"Why have we become lazy and apathetic?"

How have ***"We the People"*** gotten ourselves into this mess? What is keeping us from waking up and doing the right thing? Why are we not willing to become engaged and to force the changes that deep down we know are much needed? Why have we become lazy and apathetic? Will we wait to take action until after it is too late? At what point will it have become too late? Where will we find national leaders who have the courage to lead us out of our denial and current bondage to debt? These are all very difficult questions, *yet there are answers.*

What *"We the People"* Need Is a "National Intervention"

Most of us are familiar with the concept of a family intervention, in which an entire family gathers to confront a loved one about that loved one's self-destructive behavior in an effort to save him or her from certain death due to their abuse of drugs or alcohol. Very often, prior to these interventions, there has been a long-running cycle of denial for a very significant period of time on the part of *everyone* in the room. The loved one for years has denied that he or she has a problem. The family members have become "enablers" to the loved one by denying to themselves and to the world around them that the loved one has any sort of problem. That denial must first be *confronted and conquered* by *all* of the parties involved before any *real* progress can begin. Otherwise, the loved one will never be able to take the "next steps" necessary to make any progress toward recovery. Likewise, each of the family members continues to create an environment in which their loved one falls back into dependency because it is "comfortable and familiar" to them. This all sounds sick, weird, and twisted; and believe me, *it is.* You must by now be asking, *"What does this story of addiction in a family have to do with what's wrong with America?"*

AMERICA'S DEBT ADDICTION

The answer to the above question is really quite simple: *America is addicted to debt.* *"We the People"* of the United States are the family members, and our loved one, in this case America, is addicted to debt. And just as in the case of a drug or alcohol addiction, *all* parties are in denial. Nobody wants to be the first to admit that we *all* have a problem. We have *all* become very comfortable living beyond our means. Besides, facing the problem will require that we must *do something to fix it*. Oh, but you might say that the politicians and the talking heads on television speak about debt all of the time in our constant public debate. Yes, they do; however, they speak of it in a sort of abstract sense with an implied acceptance that the debt really doesn't matter. In fact, our recent vice president, Dick Cheney, made the statement a short while back that "deficits don't matter."

> *"deficits **do** matter. Debt **does** matter. Living beyond your means **does** have consequences. There **will** be a day of reckoning."*

Well, as much as I hate to be the person to tell everyone, deficits *do* matter. Debt *does* matter. Living beyond your means *does* have consequences. There *will* be a day of reckoning. We saw the reality of this most recently in the case of the mortgage meltdown. We then saw it play out again in the failure of the auto industry. But have you noticed what *really* occurred? What *really* occurred is that *"We the People"* didn't truly face *either* of these problems. Instead, we continued the denial of our addiction by simply adding more debt to *both* of them. When it became obvious that fundamental financial rules had been broken and that we must now face the consequences, *"We the People"* chose to deny the reality of the problem and to once again delay the inevitable. Instead of admitting the real problem and doing the right thing, *"We the People"* chose to postpone facing reality by simply borrowing *more* money. We chose to transfer these failures from the private sector to the public sector by piling mountains of debt onto the backs of future generations of the American people. As a result of living in denial, we now have state-run banks, state-run insurance companies, and state-run automobile manufacturing companies. This is all *socialism,* and it is *un-American*. Much of it is very likely *unconstitutional*. To put it mildly, our founders would *not* be pleased. Once again, we have dishonored the sacrifices of the founders of our great nation by virtue of our reckless and illegal actions. Thomas Jefferson reminded us not to run up large debt obligations:

"I say, the earth belongs to each of these generations during its course, fully and in its own right. The second generation receives it clear of the debts and incumbrances of the first, the third of the second, and so on. For if the first could charge it with a debt, then the earth would belong to the dead and not to the living generation. Then, no generation can contract debts greater than may be paid during the course of its own existence."

—**Thomas Jefferson** in a letter to James Madison,
September 6, 1789

"The leaders of our national government, by their own actions, have trained each of us to live beyond our means."

"**We the People**" of the United States are in a national denial, and we are in *desperate* need of an intervention. Not one of us should be surprised that so many of our citizens have gotten themselves into serious financial trouble. All that is required to figure this one out is to look at who has been setting the example for our citizens. The leaders of our national government, by their own actions, have *trained* each of us to live beyond our means. In many cases, they have not only taught us by their own example to live beyond our means, they have also actively encouraged us to do so! For example, our national leaders instructed both Fannie Mae and Freddie Mac to make "no-money-down" home loans to a great many people in this country so those people would buy homes that they actually could *not afford* and had *no business* buying in the first place. Our nationally elected leaders in the U.S. Congress, with a more-than-willing accomplice in the president of the United States, have run our nation into a bottomless abyss of debt and into national bankruptcy.

Meanwhile, "**We the People**" have stood by and *allowed* it to happen. We could have stopped it, but we didn't. So ask yourself a question: "Would you in your wildest dreams ever have allowed your wife, your husband, your sister, or your brother to go down to the local bank to borrow endless amounts of money *in your name*, thereby forcing you into personal bankruptcy?" If not, why then have *you* allowed your national government to do the exact same thing to you? Driving you into personal bankruptcy is precisely what you have allowed the government to do to you. You have actually done it to yourself, for "**We the People**" *are* the government. Are you prepared to take any action against this in the future, or are you now willing to allow your elected leaders to go forward with bankrupting your children and your children's children? You and I are totally responsible for what has occurred in our nation, and we are likewise totally responsible for bringing it to an end. The buck stops with "*We the People*." "De'Nial" is not just a river in Egypt. Denial is where you and I have been living while we have allowed our national leaders to recklessly drive our country into national bankruptcy. So there is your intervention. There is your reality check.

Is There Any Good News Here?
Yes, *"We the People"* Can Fix This

> "'*We the People*' *have a very solemn obligation to right these wrongs. It must be done, and it must be done very soon.*"

In the opinion of this farmer from Indiana, *"We the People"* *can* redeem ourselves from the mistakes of our past. We *can* take control of our nation's future and put ourselves back on a strong, solid footing. It won't be easy, though. Nothing worthwhile is ever easy. However, the payoff will be *more* than worth the effort. The payoff will be that we will have secured the future of our great nation. The payoff will be that we will be honoring the sacrifices of our founders. The payoff will be that we will leave our children and our grandchildren the same birthright that was given us and that we have been so blessed to enjoy during *our* lifetimes. Make no mistake: it is incumbent upon each one of us that we honor the sacrifices of our founders. More important, we *must* leave the gift of our great democratic experiment with the same secure future that it had when we inherited it from those people who came before us. As Thomas Jefferson would say, "*It is our right, it is our duty.*" In point of fact, *"We the People"* have a very *solemn obligation* to right these wrongs. *It must* be done, and it must be done *very soon*. In this book, you will find the specific action plans necessary to allow us to once again make things right, to redeem our great God-given gifts of Liberty and Freedom, and to secure those gifts for future generations of Americans.

> "even if '*We the People*' had not already decided that our experiment with socialism should end, the inherent financial limitations have brought it all crashing down around our ears anyway."

It is interesting that at *precisely* the same moment in time that "**We the People**" have finally endured enough of government at every level getting bigger and more repressive of our rights as citizens, that the ultimate financial limitations of government's excessive growth through borrowing have also reared their ugly heads, *forcing* us to take action. In other words, even if "**We the People**" had not already decided that our experiment with socialism should end, the inherent financial limitations have brought it all crashing down around our ears anyway. Perhaps we needed both our own realization and the inevitable financial limitations to occur simultaneously in order for us to face reality and be brought to our senses. Either way, we have arrived at a point in time where we are left with *no choice* other than to face the fact that *we are broke*. This is really no different than what occurred in the Soviet Union in the last century. America was able to win the cold war against the Soviets because our capitalistic, free enterprise economy granted us the luxury of being able to "outspend" them militarily. As long as America maintained the tenets of Freedom and Liberty, our economy could easily out-produce the Soviet Union and eventually drive them into bankruptcy. The Soviets simply couldn't afford both "guns and butter". No nation can afford both—not even the United States of America. Our current financial dilemma is really nothing more than a "delayed version" of what brought down the Soviet Union. America has now reached the limits of her own ability to spend and borrow any additional money. Attempting to sustain and further expand socialism in America is now entirely out of the question and no longer an option for America. Continuing this reckless spending and advance toward socialism equates to forfeiting our great American Republic and, along with it, our very way of life.

> *"If we fail to repair this fiscal mess… ours will be a generation of leaving a legacy of sowing the seeds that will lead to America's demise."*

Make no mistake: "**We the People**" *will* rise above this crisis. We have overcome graver calamities, such as the Civil War, World War I, and World War II. Repairing this mistake will require great sacrifice, but none more difficult or burdensome than those endured by the brave generations of Americans who have preceded us. Each and every one of those earlier generations have left our beloved American nation better off than when they received it from the prior generation. We can and *we must* do no different. If we fail to repair this fiscal mess that *we* have created and not restore our unique American Freedom and Liberty, ours will be a generation of leaving a legacy of sowing the seeds that will lead to America's demise. That outcome is *totally and utterly unacceptable.* As a citizen, I look forward to the challenge of repairing America. It will be a rewarding and gratifying experience. The process will reawaken the sense that, together, we can overcome anything simply because we are, after all, *Americans.* It will require us to once again focus on the fundamental principles that made America the miracle that it was on the day of its founding. These principles ensure that America was then and still remains even in our day, *The last best hope for man on earth.*

> *"There is no reason to ever allow our federal government spending to exceed 20 percent of our gross domestic product."*

Annual U.S. government spending doubled in less than ten years between the years 2000 and 2009. It grew from consuming 33 percent of the U.S. gross domestic product (GDP; the gross domestic product is the sum total of all the goods and services produced by a nation in any given year) to 45 percent of the U.S. GDP in that same period. During the depression and throughout the entire decade of the 1930s, federal government spending only comprised around 20 percent of GDP. Prior to the 1930s, U.S. government spending was typically less than 10 percent of GDP. During just the last one-third (1/3) of our existence as a nation, "**We the People**" have allowed the government to grow by over *400 percent* and consistently consume 45 percent of the nation's economy! Your elected leaders have led you down this path slowly and very insidiously over a period of seventy or eighty years. We now must ask ourselves, at what point will "**We the People**" wake up some morning having completely relinquished *all* of our Freedom and Liberty to government? My friends, we have *already* arrived at that point. There is no reason to ever allow our federal government spending to exceed 20 percent of our gross domestic product.

> *"The balanced budget requirement and 20 percent of GDP cap must be mandated by law for U.S. government spending."*

It needs to be the goal of our nation to *immediately* reduce and eliminate U.S. federal government spending, put in place a balanced budget requirement by amending the U.S. Constitution, and along with it, adopt an additional requirement that limits federal government spending to 20 percent of U.S. gross domestic product. After all, forty-nine states *already* have a balanced budget requirement! The balanced budget requirement and 20 percent of GDP cap must be *mandated by law* for U.S. government spending. The only very rare exception will be during times of war, and then only to allow spending to be out of balance or increase beyond 20 percent of GDP for that part of the federal spending that is *directly attributable* to the cost of the war. This is all simply common sense. In the long run, the federal government is subject to the exact same economic limitations as you and I. There is no escaping these fundamental laws of finance. Do you think for one minute if your author, this farmer from Indiana, had operated his farm and his business on the same basis that your federal officials have operated your government, that he would still have a business to operate or be living on his farm today? We all know the answer to that question.

> *"We have now reached a moment in time when the future of our very Republic is at stake. Complacency is no longer an option. If we do not act, and act now, we will all wake up one morning, scratch our heads, and wonder what went wrong. But it will be too late at that point. Your government will be making all of your decisions for you..."*

Why do we allow the federal government to perpetually break these laws of economics and finance? It is only because **"We the People"** have, up to now, chosen to do nothing about it. Unfortunately, **"We the People"** no longer have the luxury of being able to further delay or procrastinate on the matter. We have now reached a moment in time when the future of our very Republic is at stake. Complacency is no longer an option. If we do not act, and *act now*, we will all wake up one morning, scratch our heads, and wonder what went wrong. But it will be too late at that point. Your government will be making *all* of your decisions for you, and they will do it because a "national financial emergency" requires it. They will blame it on the economy or on terrorism or on anything other than their own mismanagement of your U.S. government. Your Freedom and Liberty will be forever lost, and you will be left with no one and no circumstance to blame except your *own failure* to exercise your God-given right to vote and to become engaged. So yes, we *can* fix this; however, it requires that **"We the People"** take action and that we take action *very soon*.

> *"Republics are created by the virtue, public spirit, and intelligence of the citizens. They fall, when the wise are banished from the public councils, because they dare to be honest, and the profligate are rewarded, because they flatter the people, in order to betray them."*
>
> --Joseph Story, Commentaries on the Constitution, 1833

CHAPTER THREE

THE UNITED STATES IS IN HEAP BIG FINANCIAL TROUBLE

"As a very important source of strength and security, cherish public credit. One method of preserving it is to use it as sparingly as possible."

—George Washington, President of the United States
From his farewell address, September 17, 1796
Born in 1732, Washington died in 1799.

> *"The total financial obligations of the federal government now represent three hundred thousand dollars ($300,000) for every man, woman, and child in the United States, or $1 million ($1,000,000) for each and every household in the United States."*

Just since early 2009, the U.S. federal government has taken over and is running much of the banking industry, much of the insurance industry, and much of the auto industry. Politicians in Washington DC now have their sights set on taking over and running the *entire* U.S. health care industry. The United States of American now has more than $15 trillion of debt that we admit to owing and upon which we pay interest. In addition to that, depending upon whom you ask, the United States has another $100 trillion or more of unfunded Social Security, Medicare, and Medicaid liabilities. The total financial obligations of the federal government now represent three hundred thousand dollars ($300,000) for *every man, woman, and child* in the United States, or $1 million ($1,000,000) for *each and every household* in the United States. Our future budget forecasts, even under very rosy and very favorable economic growth estimates, are shown to include annual budget deficits of more than $1 trillion each year for the next several years. Despite all of this, our federal representatives are now taking steps to create even larger mountains of debt by blindly marching into a black hole of guaranteeing health care for every American citizen and illegal immigrant. The credit card of the United States has reached its limit. Do yourself a favor. Go to www.usdebtclock.org on the Internet. Be ready for a major shock to your system.

THE PARTY IS OVER

America is not *going* broke. America is by every reasonable measure actually *already bankrupt*. All that is left for *"We the People"* to do is to administer the reorganization in that bankruptcy. The jig is up for us. We have reached a point in time where our nation is left with no alternative but to begin a massive reorganization of our government. There is simply *no way* going forward that the U.S. government can honor the obligations she has to each of her citizens; nor can she keep the promises she has made to her creditors. *"We the People"* *must* get our financial affairs in order, and *time is short*. Any further delay in making the changes needed will very likely result in *"killing the goose that lays the golden eggs"*—our national economy and ultimately our very system of government. If we long continue our past behavior into the future, *"We the People"* will choose to administer this bankruptcy reorganization by virtue of either defaulting on our debt obligations or creating hyperinflation through the unlimited printing of money, or by some combination of these two. Neither of these two options should be acceptable to any of us.

> *"we must put forward a plan that honors our past and provides a secure legacy for our future."*

In our reorganization, we must pledge to ourselves as well as to our creditors that *"We the People"* will *not* default on our obligations either by avoiding payment or by creating massive inflation. Instead, we must set things right. Just like an individual or business entity, *"We the People"* must liquidate our nation's assets, pay our debts, and begin to live within our collective means. While we are in this bankruptcy liquidation and reorganization, we must also simultaneously reorganize our national government to prevent this from ever again occurring in our future. The first step in this process is to pledge to one another that we will *no longer* continue to further burden tomorrow's American citizens with our sins of overindulgence today. Second, we must put forward a plan that honors our past and provides a secure legacy for our future. Third, we must get busy about implementing the reorganization plan; and we must do it sooner rather than later.

ALL THINGS ARE POSSIBLE

> *"The real threat or enemy to America is an out-of-control federal government that has been taken over by elitist career politicians who are, at heart, socialists."*

Despite all of these very sobering facts, if we act quickly and decisively, *"We the People"* *can* save this nation's financial future. People often forget, or perhaps they just take for granted, that the United States of America has the most prosperous economy on the face of the earth. A resilient capitalistic free enterprise system is difficult to negatively affect.

In fact, despite our constant and repeated past abuses of it, the economy of the United States has *always* managed to rebound and come back even stronger and more dynamic than ever. That history is the living testament of the merits of a free-market economy. It will take more than a few mistakes in mortgage lending to put the American economy on its knees. Besides, the real threat to America is *not* the recent financial crisis. The *real* threat or enemy to America is an out-of-control federal government that has been taken over by elitist, career politicians who are, at heart, *socialists*. This current crisis, while severe, should be viewed as our final wake-up call to take the much-needed action in our government that has been long overdue.

"I wish it were possible to obtain a single amendment to our Constitution. I would be willing to depend on that alone for the reduction of the administration of our government to the genuine principles of its Constitution; I mean an additional article, taking from the federal government the power of borrowing."

—**Thomas Jefferson,** in a letter to John Taylor, November 26, 1798

ON BAILOUTS AND "SO-CALLED" ECONOMIC STIMULUS

"Congress called the bailout 'TARP' for 'Troubled Asset Recovery Program.' Actually, this made perfect sense to farmers from Indiana, for we have always known that one uses a tarp to 'cover things up.'"

"Were we directed from Washington when to sow & when to reap, we should soon want bread."

—Thomas Jefferson, *date unknown*

In September 2008, the U.S. stock market began to get wobbly and fluctuate wildly. By the end of September, word came out that certain financial institutions in the United States had become insolvent. President George W. Bush and Secretary of the Treasury Henry Paulson announced that they would be recommending to the Congress that ***"We the People"*** spend $700 billion on a bailout of certain U.S. financial institutions by virtue of buying what they described as "toxic assets" that were held by these financial institutions. Congress called the bailout "TARP" for "Troubled Asset Recovery Program." Actually, this name made perfect sense to farmers from Indiana, for we have always known that one uses a tarp to *"cover things up."* After first being voted down due to a loud clamor of protests from ***"We the People,"*** Congress voted a second time and ultimately passed the bill.

As it turned out, that was *only the beginning.* That event set the tone and paved the way for the passing of many more spending bills in the Congress over the next few months under both Presidents Bush and Obama, which culminated in a massive $787 billion economic stimulus bill that was rammed through the Congress with not so much as a cursory review by any of the lawmakers. Added together, the U.S. government would spend not just billions, but literally *trillions* of dollars on bailouts and "stimulus" plans. This spending might have been all well and good, except for the small detail that ***"We the People"*** didn't have the trillions to spend. The money would *all* have to be *borrowed,* resulting in our mortgaging the future of this once great creditor nation to an extent that it will very likely lead to the financial demise of the United States if strong action is not taken and taken *very soon.*

THREE REASONS WHY *"WE THE PEOPLE"* SHOULD NOT BE DOING WHAT WE ARE CURRENTLY DOING

1. We very simply cannot afford what we are doing.

We are out of money. In fact, we were dead broke before all of this current insane spending began. What we are now doing is committing generational theft on our children, grandchildren, and great-grandchildren. *We* are choosing to live large and well beyond our means by borrowing money that *they* will have to repay. Make no mistake: they *will* repay this debt. It is unavoidable. Actions have consequences. Future generations will repay this money through austerity and a much lower standard of living; and they will very likely experience hyperinflation and the destruction of the U.S. currency in the process. Inflation is nothing more than a tax—an insidious, but nonetheless very real, tax. The higher the inflation rate, the higher the tax.

The United States was already in very BIG financial trouble well before the most recent round of idiotic spending began. Before the current so-called financial crisis, the U.S. had amassed $10 trillion of debt. On top of that, depending upon whom you ask, the U.S. has another $100 trillion in unfunded Social Security, Medicare, and Medicaid liabilities. We as a nation have made financial promises that we have no possible way of keeping. What we have done as a nation is very much like what the automobile companies attempted but failed to do, which ultimately bankrupted them. The only real difference between General Motors and the U.S. government's unfunded financial promises is the sheer size of the fraud. The U.S. government's Ponzi scheme makes General Motors' look like petty theft. No wonder our government thinks it is okay to bail out General Motors. In the sick and twisted logic of an elitist career politician, this somehow justifies his or her own idiotic past behavior of running our government into the ground.

For all of the reasons stated above, every American citizen should be fighting against this current insane spending with every ounce of their strength for the simple reason that we don't have the money and we cannot afford it. If that is not reason enough, then every American citizen should be fighting against this current insane spending with every ounce of their strength because it is morally wrong to *steal* from our children, our grandchildren, and our great-grandchildren. Stealing from future generations of Americans is precisely what we are doing. It is morally wrong, and it also dishonors the sacrifices made by our founders when they created this great nation of ours and entrusted it to us for safekeeping.

2. What we are doing will not work.

If the fact that we cannot afford it weren't reason enough to stop this insane spending, then fight against it for the simple reason that *it won't work.* We are spending all of this money in an effort to "paper over" bad decisions made by a whole bunch of misguided, dishonest, or stupid people, many of whom are elitist, career politicians and government bureaucrats. What we *should be* doing instead is to simply let these excesses "wring themselves out" of our economy. The pain would be severe but quick and would mostly affect only those who deserve to be affected. Instead, our current approach will mostly affect the innocent—the U.S. taxpayer and future generations of Americans. If the government wanted to do something to help the situation, they should have done the precise *opposite* of what they did. That is, they should have gotten out of the way, *reduced* government spending, and *cut* taxes. That would have stimulated the economy.

When the stack of cards began to fall in September 2008, my brother and I were on vacation overseas with our wives. We were watching all of this unfold at home in the United States on television in Europe. I will never forget my brother rhetorically asking, *"Why is the government spending $700 billion on this? Won't someone in the private sector be willing to step up and buy these 'toxic assets'?"* Brother Tim was right on in his assessment. Yes indeed, any number of strong companies would have looked for an opportunity to profit and would have absorbed these assets, for better or for worse. In fact, many did. For example, Bank of America bought Countrywide Home Loan and Merrill Lynch, and so on. That is how capitalism works. The strong survive, and the weak disappear. The best course of action that the U.S. federal government could have taken would have been to *do nothing,* take absolutely no action whatsoever. Instead, our elected leaders chose to make matters worse. They repeated the same mistakes of the 1930s by stepping in, throwing good money after bad money, and piling needless debt onto the backs of the American people. This will result in unnecessarily prolonging the pain.

"To contract new debts is not the way to pay old ones."
—George Washington to James Welch, April 7, 1799

A personal story to illustrate this point ...

I was fortunate enough to serve on the board of a community bank for more than a decade and learned a great deal from some very wise and successful people. John Benjamin Good led the bank that his grandfather founded in 1883. Ben was from "the Greatest Generation" and understood very well the importance of certain eternal concepts like honesty, trust, prudence, and good stewardship. What is even more important, Ben *lived* those values every day of his life. Ben would *never* have been a party to creating a mess like we have now because he stuck to what worked. Ben stuck to fundamental principles that have worked for all time—principles like loaning money only to people who have the ability to repay the money and requiring that they have some "vested interest" in the form of a down payment, and so on. Ben understood that part of his job was to keep people from getting into financial trouble. Sometimes that meant literally protecting them from themselves. By that I mean protecting them from their own tendency to "overreach" financially or to pursue greed. Ben knew these actions could lead to disaster for them, for the bank, and for the depositors of the bank.

Ben would not hesitate to remind customers, loan officers, members of the loan committee, and bank board members that *"this is not our money, we are simply stewards."* Ben Good would not have "thrown good money at a bad loan." When there were bad loans, Ben took his losses and moved on, knowing that if you stick to the right principles in making loans, you won't have very many losses. Ben would say that when you do have losses, you should learn from them and accept them, but under no circumstance should you ever expect others to bail you out of your own bad decision. There is no doubt that if Ben Good were living today, he would be shocked and stunned at what the U.S. government is doing in response to this financial crisis. These current politicians need to be relieved of their power and replaced before our great nation is damaged beyond repair.

> *"You cannot spend your way out of a recession or borrow your way out of debt. And when you repeat, in that wooden and perfunctory way, that our situation is better than others, that we are well placed to weather the storm, I have to tell you, you sound like a Brezhnev-era apparatchik giving the party line. You know and we know and you know that we know that it's nonsense.*

Everyone knows that Britain is worse off than any other country as we go into these hard times. The IMF has said so. The European Commission has said so. The markets say so, which is why the pound has lost a third of its value. In a few months, the voters will have their chance to say so, too. They can see what the markets have seen: that you are the devalued Prime Minister of a devalued Government."

—**Daniel Hannan,** a member of the European Parliament,
to Prime Minister Gordon Brown on March 24, 2009

"Man cannot make principles; he can only discover them."

—**Thomas Paine,** *The Age of Reason,* 1794

3. What we are doing is un-American.

"We do absolutely no one a favor and everyone a tremendous disservice by trying to 'paper over' our own bad behavior ... it is absolutely unfair, and yes un-American, to ask millions of average American taxpayers to pay for reckless mistakes made by a very few greedy, stupid, or unwise individuals."

In #1 above, we reviewed why we can't afford what we are doing. In #2 above, we reviewed why what we are doing will not work. I would like now to provide you with what is perhaps the most important reason of all why you need to fight with every ounce of your strength against what our government is doing. *It is un-American.* What we are doing as a nation is counter to and goes against what made the United States the greatest nation to have ever existed. We do absolutely no one a favor and everyone a tremendous disservice by trying to "paper over" our own bad behavior. Besides, it is absolutely unfair, and yes un-American, to ask millions of average American taxpayers to pay for reckless mistakes made by a very few greedy, stupid, or unwise individuals. Oh, but the politicians will tell you that we can't let these banks and financial institutions fail, for it will cause a financial Armageddon in America. So what's their point? That is what capitalism is all about. With capitalism, there are winners and losers.

We are going to have to take our medicine for these poor decisions sooner or later. Let's get it over with! Let the chips fall where they may. Sure, there will be pain, but at least *most* of the pain will be visited upon those people and those institutions that *deserve* the pain.

> *"A true capitalistic system, if left alone, will heal itself remarkably fast."*

It is both interesting and sad how quickly we have forgotten what made this nation, the United States of America, the greatest economic powerhouse in the history of man. We have experienced *many* recessions and depressions in our nation's history. In each and every case, we have recovered, and our economy has gone on to grow bigger and stronger than ever before. A true capitalistic system, if left alone, will heal itself remarkably fast. It is only when we attempt to intervene that we get ourselves into trouble and prolong the agony. The Great Depression of the 1930s is the best example of what *not* to do. That depression could have remained a recession if the U.S. government had not intervened with exactly the wrong measures. Rather than spend time going into the evidence that proves this statement, I will refer you to a book titled *The Forgotten Man: A New History of the Great Depression* by Amity Shlaes.

> *"I would submit to you that the only citizens who are un-American are people just like Nancy Pelosi."*

In 2009 the United States Speaker of the House of Representatives, Nancy Pelosi, characterized the behavior of thousands of concerned American citizens as "un-American" because these folks were showing up at town hall meetings with questions about the federal government's attempt to "take over" the entire health care delivery system in the United States. I would submit to you that the only citizens who are un-American are people *just like* Nancy Pelosi. One hundred seventy years ago, Davey Crockett made this case better than I or anyone else could. So with that said, I would like to share with you a public story that proves my above claim that the recent action by the U.S. government is un-American.

THE "NOT YOURS TO GIVE" SPEECH
DAVEY CROCKETT'S VIEW OF THE U.S. CONSTITUTION

**David Crockett, *"King of the Wild Frontier"*
Born in Tennessee in 1786
Died at the battle of the Alamo in Texas on March 6, 1836**

"We have rights, as individuals, to give as much of our own money as we please to charity; but as members of Congress, we have no right so to appropriate a dollar of public money."

—**David Crockett,** U.S. Congressman (1827–1835)

Everyone has heard the legend of Davey Crockett, an American folk hero, frontiersman, and soldier. But few know that he served as a U.S. Congressman from Tennessee from 1827 until 1835 before he gave his life defending Freedom at the Battle of the Alamo in 1836. The following excerpt, reprinted from an 1884 book with the title *The Life of Colonel David Crockett*, by Edward S. Ellis, illustrates the true meaning of the U.S. Constitution simply and elegantly. Davey Crockett understood what our unique American government is to be about—much better than today's self-serving, elitist, career politicians do.

One day in the U.S. House of Representatives, a bill was taken up appropriating money for the benefit of a widow of a distinguished naval officer. Several beautiful speeches had been made in its support. The Speaker was just about to put the question when Davey Crockett arose [and said]:

> *"Mr. Speaker, I have as much respect for the memory of the deceased, and as much sympathy for the sufferings of the living, if suffering there be, as any man in this House, but we must not permit our respect for the dead or our sympathy for a part of the living to lead us into an act of injustice to the balance of the living. I will not go into an argument to prove that Congress has no power to appropriate this money as an act of charity. Every member upon this floor knows it. We have the right, as individuals, to give away as much of our own money as we please in charity; but as members of Congress, we have no right to appropriate a dollar of the public money. Some eloquent appeals have been made to us upon the ground that it is a debt due the deceased. Mr. Speaker, the deceased lived long after the close of the war; he was in office to the day of his death, and I have never heard that the government was in arrears to him. Every man in this House knows it is not a debt. We cannot, without the grossest corruption, appropriate this money as the payment of a debt. We have not the semblance of authority to appropriate it as a charity. Mr. Speaker, I have said we have the right to give as much money of our own as we please. I am the poorest man on this floor. I cannot vote for this bill, but I will give one week's pay to the object, and, if every member of Congress will do the same, it will amount to more than the bill asks."*

Crockett took his seat. Nobody replied. The bill was put upon its passage, and, instead of passing unanimously, as was generally supposed, and as, no doubt, it would, but for that speech, it received but few votes, and of course, was lost. Later, Crockett commented:

> *"There is one thing now to which I will call your attention. You remember that I proposed to give a week's pay. There are in that House many very wealthy men—men who*

think nothing of spending a week's pay, or a dozen of them, for a dinner or a wine party when they have something to accomplish by it. Some of those same men made beautiful speeches upon the great debt of gratitude which the country owed the deceased—a debt that could not be paid by money—and the insignificance and worthlessness of money, particularly so insignificant a sum as $10,000, when weighed against the honor of the nation. Yet not one of them responded to my proposition. Money with them is nothing but trash when it is to come out of the people. But it is the one great thing for which most of them are striving, and many of them sacrifice honor, integrity, and justice to obtain it."

"The consequences of our choosing to ignore the Constitution have brought us right up to the precipice of losing the very Republic for which it was written. Will you stand by and be a party to 'killing the goose that lays the golden eggs'?"

It is not the function of the national government to make direct transfer payments to individual citizens, and it is in no way provided for in the Constitution. Davey Crockett knew this and was not afraid to remind others. Our exceptional document, the U.S. Constitution, has not changed in this regard since those days of Davey Crockett. All that has changed has been our current elected leaders' willingness to abide by it. During the last third of our existence as a nation, most of our nationally elected leaders have demonstrated that they clearly lack an understanding of and an appreciation for the U.S. Constitution. The time has arrived for us to meet our obligations in this regard. *"We the People"* are on shaky ground with respect to this issue. The consequences of our choosing to ignore the Constitution have brought us right up to the precipice of losing the very Republic for which it was written. Will you stand by and be a party to *"killing the goose that lays the golden eggs"*? Or will you stand up, be counted, get engaged, and choose a different course? Fortunately, based upon the springing up of the Tea Party movement all across America since 2009, I am encouraged that *"We the People"* are now starting to wake up.

> *"It is not the function of the government to keep the citizen from falling into error; it is the function of the citizen to keep the government from falling into error."*
>
> —**Supreme Court Justice Robert H. Jackson** in 1950
> (Born February 13, 1892, Jackson died October 9, 1954.)

On National Health Care

"Our nation has clearly been hijacked by socialists."

We have this entire issue exactly backward, completely upside down. We have forgotten who we are and what has made us so great as a nation. We must return to what works. We must have the courage to turn away from what we know does not work. In 2009, we saw our European friends turning away from socialism and transitioning back toward Freedom, Liberty, capitalism, and free enterprise. These are all of the principles upon which we were able to build our nation into the greatest economic miracle the world has ever witnessed. These principles are literally in our "national DNA." Why are we choosing to move away from these principles by nationalizing much of our private enterprise companies and industries? Shouldn't we be doing precisely the opposite? Shouldn't we be *privatizing* government-run entities such as the Post Office and Amtrak? Why don't we put the U.S. Post Office up for bid to successful companies like FedEx or UPS and sell Amtrak to successful privately held railroad companies? The behavior of our nation these past few years makes absolutely no sense, given the history and experience of the United States. Our nation has clearly been hijacked by socialists.

> *"Let us first allow the federal government to prove that they can be successful at something before we give them any new responsibilities, most especially the responsibility for something that comprises one-sixth of the U.S. economy! What are we thinking?"*

As this is being written, ***"We the People"*** are in the process of debating the handover of the entire health care industry in the United States to a group of people who have proven beyond any reasonable doubt that they are completely and totally incapable of operating Social

Security, Medicare, Medicaid, and legions of other programs on an efficient and profitable basis. The health care industry represents 16 percent, or one-sixth of the entire U.S. economy, and yet we are about to turn it over to an entity that in 2008 *alone* allowed Medicare, Medicaid, and Social Security to be defrauded of an estimated $100 billion. What an indictment! Let us first allow the federal government to prove that they can be successful at something before we give them any new responsibilities, most especially the responsibility for something that comprises one-sixth of the U.S. economy! What are we thinking? These people have created $100 trillion of financial liabilities that taxpayers of the United States are responsible to meet and have driven us into national bankruptcy. The total federal government debt for our national liabilities now represents three hundred thousand dollars ($300,000) for *every man, woman, and child* in the United States, or $1 million ($1,000,000) for *each and every household* in the United States. This type of insane behavior by our elected leaders on behalf of the American people needs to come to an abrupt end, not be expanded into an entirely new area!

The Obama administration early in 2009 began by estimating the cost to the American taxpayer for the takeover of the health care industry at around $650 billion. Democrat Representative Chris Van Hollen of Maryland appeared on *Fox News* on June 25, 2009, and said that the cost will likely exceed $1 trillion. According to the "U.S. House Discussion Draft" of June 19, 2009, the cost to taxpayers for national health care will be $3.5 trillion over ten years. Whether one is building a home or planning a project, we all know that the estimated cost for anything is always low as compared to the actual final costs. However, in the case of the United States nationalizing health care, it really doesn't matter whether the final cost will be $650 billion, $1 trillion, or $3.5 trillion, or more. *"We the People"* cannot afford *any* amount of new spending or debt. What we seem to be forgetting is that *we are dead BROKE!* Is there any reason to point out that if we turn our health care over to the federal government that we are virtually guaranteed that the cost of health care will go way up and the quality and availability will precipitously drop? Need I say more? Probably not, for this issue falls under Point #8 of Our 2nd American Revolution anyway. Point #8 is this: *"We the People"* do hereby put the United States Congress and the U.S. President on notice that they are to immediately *cease and desist* from any further "nationalization" of the private sector of the U.S. economy or intervention into the lives and property of *"We the People."*

Update: On March 23, 2010, President Barack Obama signed The Patient Protection and Affordable Care Act, or "Obama Care" into law. However, with more than half of the American people wanting it repealed, the survival of this law is in doubt. The constitutionality of the legislation will be heard before the Supreme Court in 2012. No matter the Supreme Court's decision, newly elected leaders of ***"We the People"*** will attempt to repeal this law in 2013. Hopefully, the success of these efforts will serve as the final epitaph on the failure of socialism in America

> *"The greatest tyrannies are always perpetrated in the name of the noblest causes."*
>
> —Thomas Paine

On Compassion

What is compassion? Who are the compassionate among us? We would all agree that Mother Teresa was compassionate. Is compassion defined as 50 percent of people being enslaved to a life of servitude in order to support the other 50 percent of the people, who are enslaved to a life of dependency? If so, you define compassion as 50 percent of the population working very hard, producing lots of goods and services, making lots of money, and paying 50 percent or more of their income in taxes, while the other 50 percent of the population work very little, produce relatively little, earn very little, and pay little or no taxes. *Or* is compassion defined as creating an environment in which people are *free* to pursue their own goals and dreams, succeed at a level of their own choosing, earn as little or as much as they want, pay as few or as many taxes as they choose? Which of our two major political parties would you say has more compassion? I would submit that *neither* of them fits the description. I prefer to define compassion as creating an environment in which people are *free* to pursue their own goals and dreams, succeed at a level of their own choosing, earn as little or as much as they desire, pay as few or as many taxes as they choose, and *be free* to help their fellow man. I believe a life of enslavement, whether it is enslavement to a life of dependency or to a life of servitude, is wrong, yet that's the life we Americans are living today.

This quote by the late Adrian Rogers perfectly explains the concept of the "tipping point," which is the point at which the producers in a society become outnumbered in the voting booth by the non-producers.

It is at this point in time when all democratic, capitalistic, free enterprise societies go into decline and ultimately disappear. These societies tend to last for a period on either side of 200 years, as explained further below by Alexander Fraser Tytler (1747–1813). Would anyone like to hazard a guess where America stands on the 200-year timeline?

> *"You cannot legislate the poor into freedom by legislating the wealthy out of freedom. What one person receives without working for, another person must work for without receiving. The government cannot give to anybody anything that the government does not first take from somebody else. When half of the people get the idea that they do not have to work because the other half is going to take care of them, and when the other half gets the idea that it does no good to work because somebody else is going to get what they work for, that my dear friend, is about the end of any nation. You cannot multiply wealth by dividing it."*
>
> —**Dr. Adrian Rogers**, Southern Baptist minister, 1931–2005

John Adams was of the opinion that *"elections, especially of representatives and counselors, should be annual … These great men … should be [chosen] once a year—Like bubbles on the sea of matter bourne, they rise, they break, and to the sea return. This will teach them the great political virtues of humility, patience, and moderation, without which every man in power becomes a ravenous beast of prey."*

Abraham Lincoln humbly and candidly admitted, *"if our American society and United States government are overthrown, it will come from the voracious desire for office, this [desire] to live without toil, work, and labor … from which I am not free myself."*

"Rulers, surely, even the most dignified and powerful of them, should not be so elevated with the thoughts of their power, as to forget from whom it comes; for what purposes it is delegated to them."

–Rev. Jonathan Mayhew,
Election Sermon, 1754.

"Governments destitute of energy, will ever produce anarchy."

—James Madison
in a speech to the Virginia Convention, June 7, 1788

"When a man assumes a public trust, he should consider himself as public property."

—Thomas Jefferson,
remarking to Baron von Humboldt, date unknown

Jonathan Mayhew, who lived from October 8, 1720, to July 9, 1766, was a noted American clergyman and minister.

"Power tends to corrupt, and absolute power corrupts absolutely."

—Lord Acton, 1887

A Thought-Provoking Story from the Time of Our Founding

The following has been attributed to Alexander Fraser Tytler (1747–1813), a Scottish-born lawyer and writer at about the time that our original thirteen states adopted their new Constitution in 1787; however, according to Snopes. com—www.snopes.com/politics/ballot/athenian.asp—it is unclear who actually authored the work.

The story is about the fall of the Athenian Republic some 2,000 years earlier:

> *A democracy is always temporary in nature; it simply cannot exist as a permanent form of government.*
>
> *A democracy will continue to exist up until the time that voters discover they can vote themselves generous gifts from the public treasury.*
>
> *From that moment on, the majority always vote for the candidates who promise the most benefits from the public treasury, with the result that every democracy will finally collapse due to loose fiscal policy, which is always followed by a dictatorship.*
>
> *The average age of the world's greatest civilizations, from the beginning of history, has been about 200 years.*
>
> *During those 200 years, the democratic nations always progressed through the following sequence:*
>
> *1. From bondage to spiritual faith;*
>
> *2. From spiritual faith to great courage;*
>
> *3. From courage to Liberty;*
>
> *4. From Liberty to abundance;*
>
> *5. From abundance to complacency;*
>
> *6. From complacency to apathy;*
>
> *7. From apathy to dependence;*
>
> *8. From dependence back into bondage.*

To the reader: I have added the timeline below. It corresponds with the eight sequential steps from above:

WHERE THE UNITED STATES OF AMERICA
FITS ON THE ABOVE TIMELINE:

1. From bondage to spiritual faith:
—*English Pilgrims begin to settle in Jamestown from Great Britain in 1607*

2. From spiritual faith to great courage:
—*People enjoyed religious freedom, became strong and courageous*

3. From courage to Liberty:
—*Colonists fought and won their Freedom and Liberty from 1775 to 1783*

4. From Liberty to abundance:
—*The miracle of American Freedom and capitalism from 1787 to 1900*

5. From abundance to complacency:
—*Becoming fat, dumb, and happy from 1900 to 1950s*

6. From complacency to apathy:
—*Taking the gift of freedom for granted from the 1950s to 1960s*

7. From apathy to dependence:
—*The welfare state and Socialism in America from the 1960s to today*

8. From dependence back into bondage:
–*Losing the gift of freedom entirely and moving toward a dictatorship*

No matter the original source of the above work, it is both interesting and amazing how this pattern associated with the rise and fall of democracies seems to repeat itself. Can there be any doubt that our founders in their studies of the ancient societies had discovered the same phenomenon? This would certainly explain their constant reminders to us of the need to never let down our guard against tyranny and to be constantly aware and mindful of the fragility of Liberty and Freedom. Where would you place America on the above timeline?

I estimate *"We the People"* are somewhere between dependence and back into bondage. That puts us at about 7.5! What are *you* willing to do about it? Are you willing to give up God's greatest gift to mankind—your Freedom and your Liberty?

SOLUTIONS:

1) Sell off the prime real estate of the United States and use the money to pay off our debt.

2) Move government activities from the prime real estate to other U.S. real estate in Nevada and Arizona.

3) Eliminate U.S. government programs and departments such as education, agriculture, labor, and so on.

4) Stop being the policeman of the world. Close fully half of our military bases and save billions.

5) Pass a Balanced Budget Amendment to the U.S. Constitution and a Presidential Line Item Veto.

6) Repeal the Sixteenth Amendment and eliminate the income tax.

CHAPTER FOUR

FEDERAL SPENDING, TAXATION, AND THE SIXTEENTH AMENDMENT

1913—THE BEGINNING OF THE END OF OUR AMERICAN REPUBLIC

"The Congress shall have power to lay and collect taxes on incomes, from whatever source derived, without apportionment among the several States, and without regard to any census or enumeration."

—The Sixteenth Amendment to the U.S. Constitution,
passed in 1913

Table 1 shows what happened to per capita (per person) spending by the U.S. federal government after the passage of the Sixteenth Amendment allowing the federal government to tax individuals on their incomes. Note the column on the right, which "nets out" spending on defense and interest on the debt. There was more than a *1,000%* (tenfold) increase in just twenty years! **Lesson: Give government the right to tax you, and they most certainly will do just that!**

Table 1:
Real Per Capita Federal Expenditures: 1915-1935
(In Constant 1990 Dollars)

Year	Total	Total Spending *Minus* Defense and Interest
1915	95.02	27.39
1916	83.60	22.75
1917	193.22	113.81
1918	1,067.31	518.37
1919	1,329.77	477.53
1920	390.98	170.15
1921	338.86	136.16
1922	232.95	78.62
1923	214.57	74.49
1924	194.85	70.36
1925	187.78	71.09
1926	184.80	76.57
1927	180.57	72.75
1928	186.56	79.89
1929	195.41	89.30
1930	211.13	101.81
1931	247.41	130.80
1932	286.39	183.98
1933	367.84	231.20
1934	498.88	361.02
1935	486.81	328.03

Source: *Historical Statistics of the United States from Colonial Times to 1970*, and author's calculations.

Check out how the U.S. government

went from spending <u>$25</u> per person in 1915–1916

to more than <u>$300</u> per person in just twenty years!

Would anyone like to take a guess how much the federal government currently spends *per person* in 2009, net of defense and interest? Would you believe something close to *$10,000!?* And that's on 178 million *more people!* We had 128 million people in the United States in 1935, and we have 306 million people here in 2009! That's a *4,000* percent increase per person as compared to 1933, and a *40,000* percent increase per person as compared to 1916!

44

> *"The founders studied the lessons that the past had to teach them … and unanimously agreed that no good end would come from a strong central government making decisions for people from a faraway place."*

If the founding fathers had one overriding mission when writing the U.S. Constitution, it was their desire to severely limit the power and scope of the central government. This was the one, single, solitary principle on which they *all* agreed. Even the Federalists, who favored a much stronger central government than did the other founders, understood the need to limit government's role. By 1787, everyone in the now United States of America was quite ready to live their lives unencumbered by a tyrannical government. They all desired to be left alone, and each earnestly believed that any power affecting the citizenry should be held at the *lowest possible level* in a society. Our founders also understood that the best decisions affecting people are made by the *family* or only at a very local level, where *accountability* would control. The founders studied the lessons that the past had to teach them from the societies of old (the Israelites, the Greeks, the Romans, and the Anglo-Saxons) and unanimously agreed that no good end would come from a strong central government making decisions for people from a faraway place. To put it in today's manner of speaking, they had *"been there and done that"* and were more than ready to move on.

> *"Slowly, but very insidiously, mostly over the past one hundred years, 'We the People' have lost sight of the wisdom that our founders had … and have allowed the federal government to grow exponentially."*

The founders were so steadfast in their mission to restrict the central government that they literally starved their first central government under the Articles of Confederation of any financial means to fight the Revolutionary War. While they later remedied their error when they formed our current system of government under the U.S. Constitution in 1787, the founders still never wavered from their commitment to limit the influence over the people by the federal government. Slowly, but very *insidiously*, mostly over the past one hundred years, **"We the People"** have lost sight of the wisdom that our founders had in this regard and have allowed the federal government to grow *exponentially*. One of the seminal events that can be pointed to where **"We the People"** clearly lost our way was in the passage in 1913 of the Sixteenth

Amendment to our U.S. Constitution. That amendment granted vast power to the federal government to *tax each individual citizen*. Heretofore, the federal government had gotten the bulk of its resources from the various states. Under that arrangement, the states could control the growth and power of the central government. However, after 1913, under the new Sixteenth Amendment, the federal government was able to bypass that state control and directly tax each individual citizen within those various states.

> *"as a result of the Sixteenth Amendment, 'We the People' have become that which our founders feared most."*

This change would serve from that day forward as a "blank check" on which the federal government would be allowed to grow unrestrained without any limits. This would ultimately lead to the federal government's ability to dominate and control the lives of each individual American citizen. The very thing that our founders had worked so hard to avoid, and had actually feared the most, would now come to pass. Big decisions affecting the lives of people would no longer be made on a manageable local level by families, churches, and communities so accountability could be maintained. Instead, they would be made in a faraway place by a *huge federal bureaucracy*. I believe that as a result of the Sixteenth Amendment, ***"We the People"** have become that which our founders feared most.*

THE OVAL OFFICE, MARCH 21, 1973 ...

> *"I began by telling the President that there was a cancer growing on the Presidency and that if the cancer was not removed, that the President himself would be killed by it. I also told him that it was important that this cancer be removed immediately because it was growing more deadly every day."*
>
> —**John Dean** testifying before Congress
> in the Watergate Hearings on June 25, 1973

The above is John Dean's recitation of what he had told President Nixon in the Oval Office concerning the cover-up of the break-in to Democratic Headquarters at the Watergate Hotel in Washington DC. Dean was testifying before Congress during the Watergate Hearings just three months after his meeting with Nixon.

John Dean was President Nixon's personal attorney. The cancer that Dean refers to in the above quote was the cover-up of the break-in by some "Nixon for reelection" operatives. John Dean's testimony and this analogy would become famous. Dean hoped that if he could be dramatic enough with Nixon in describing what was happening by covering up the break-in that Nixon might order all concealment efforts ended. Unfortunately for Nixon, and for America, Dean's attempt at drama failed, and ultimately President Nixon resigned from office for his participation in the Watergate cover-up. Nixon resigned in order to avoid facing an almost certain impeachment proceeding that would very likely have removed him from office.

"I heartily accept the motto `The government is best which governs least'; and I should like to see it acted up to more rapidly and systematically. Carried out, it finally amounts to this, which I also believe, `That government is best which governs not at all.'"

—**Henry David Thoreau**, 1817–1862

GOVERNMENT IS LIKE A CANCER

"Government, just like cancer, if allowed to grow exponentially and get large enough, will … eventually kill its host."

Why do I bring up John Dean's famous testimony from 1973? I bring it up because government is much like a cancer. Cancer is nothing more than cells that can't get organized and begin to grow exponentially, eventually killing the host on which it lives. Government, just like cancer, if allowed to grow exponentially and get large enough, will likewise eventually kill its host. The host on which government feeds is the nation's economic system, or the very nation itself. Government is an economic drag on an economy. The larger government spending becomes as a percentage of the gross domestic product (GDP), the bigger the drag on that economy. Allow government to grow unchecked, and like cancer, it will most assuredly overtake and, yes, *kill* its host.

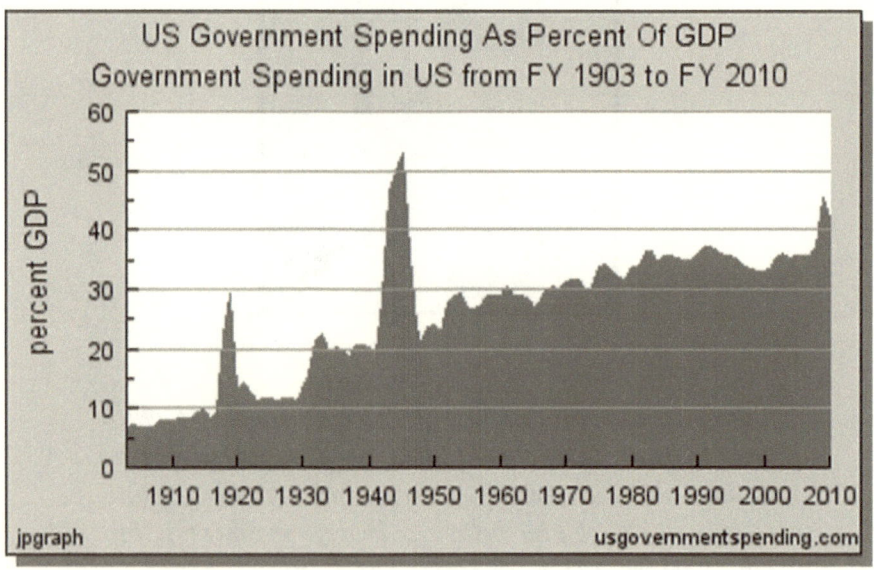

As you can see from the above graph, total spending by government as a percentage of the U.S. economy gradually grew from 6 or 7 percent of GDP to over 40 percent during the past 100 years (45 percent in 2009). Take note of the spikes for World War I, World War II, and the recent War on Terror. These "war spikes" represent the spending that our founding fathers had in mind as being the *"single primary purpose"* for the U.S. federal government. Much more important than the spikes, please take note of the overall *600 percent growth* in total government spending from around *6 to 7 percent* of GDP to currently *45 percent* in 2009. This is growth that our founders did *not* have in mind. In fact, it is what our founders feared most and warned us repeatedly would happen if we were to let down our guard and not remain vigilant about keeping the size and scope of government small and manageable.

"The natural progress of things is for liberty to yield and government to gain ground."

—**Thomas Jefferson,** in a letter to Edward Carrington,
May 27, 1788

"If we can prevent the government from wasting the labors of the people under the pretense of taking care of them, they must become happy."

—**Thomas Jefferson**, in a letter to Dr. Thomas Cooper,
Nov. 29, 1802

"Government's entire existence is totally dependent upon the people's willingness to support it."

Where does government obtain the resources needed to function, if not from the people? *Government creates nothing. Government produces nothing.* Government's entire existence is totally dependent upon the people's willingness to support it. The more resources the government is able to extract from the people, the larger and more powerful *it* becomes and the smaller and less powerful the *people* become. The beauty of all of this is that our opportunity resides in our pain. We shall simply cut the feeding tube (the tax revenue) on which the beast grows, allowing entire parts of the beast to die while at the same time beginning to tame and control all of the other parts. If we fail to do this, the beast will very definitely and very quickly consume *"We the People."*

REDUCE THE FEDERAL GOVERNMENT AND RETURN LIBERTY AND FREEDOM TO *"WE THE PEOPLE"*

The solution is that we *must* repeal the Sixteenth Amendment to the U.S. Constitution and, with it, the 66,000-page IRS income tax code. Once we have eliminated or reduced in size large pieces of the federal government, it will not be necessary to replace the income tax as a source of revenue for the national treasury. The income tax comprises 40 to 45 percent of the revenue of the federal government. That is the approximate amount of the federal government that *"We the People"* will be eliminating or turning back to the people or to the states. If there is a need for additional revenue for government, it will be for local or state governments, *not federal.* In that event, each state and local community will determine *on their own* whether they need any additional revenue.

> *"we will entirely eliminate the IRS's involvement in the lives and property of "We the People."*

The consumption or sales tax that the *"fair tax"* people have proposed to replace the income tax on a national level has merit, and local governments within each state will likely consider it. This source of raising public revenue is appealing on many levels. Revenues are easy to collect—at the time of a purchase. Most states are now collecting revenue via this format anyway in the form of state sales taxes. The best feature of this source of tax revenue for government is that it *discourages consumption* by people and *encourages thrift*. Encouraging thrift in our nation will be essential and a great thing for the people in this new era as we transition from a debtor nation back to a creditor nation. An added bonus to all of this is that we will entirely eliminate the IRS's involvement in the lives and property of *"We the People."*

The important point here is that repealing the Sixteenth Amendment to the U.S. Constitution and eliminating the IRS, replacing it with a consumption tax, should *not* be done on a "national" basis with a "national" tax, but rather with each of the individual states and local communities making these decisions on an entirely "local" level. History has clearly demonstrated, and we now know for a certainty, that any decisions affecting people on a personal basis *must* be made at the lowest possible level in the society so that *"accountability"* is possible and can be required. This will be a boon to America and give *"We the People"* great Freedom and Liberty to choose where we desire to live and how we choose to be governed. It will create an atmosphere in which *each person* can decide how much government involvement *they want* in their lives.

> *""We the People" will create a society in which all Americans have Freedom and Liberty that for the past one hundred years have been unimaginable."*

If people desire that their government provide them more services, even including providing for their health care needs, they may choose to live in a state that provides a great array of state-run services and thereby pay a correspondingly high tax rate on their consumption. Likewise, if people desire a more limited governmental influence in their lives and choose to be more self-reliant, they can live in a state with low taxes and *be free* to provide services on their own. This system will create an environment in which states and communities will actually *compete* for where *"We the People"* live and work. It will generate efficiencies on a scale that would never be possible in a "one-size-fits-all" national system. This Federalism honors the original plan of our founders, and it also gives each individual American tremendous Freedom and Liberty. Just imagine; *"We the People"* will create a society in which all Americans have Freedom and Liberty that for the past one hundred years have been unimaginable.

> *"'Reaganomics'" worked so well that it resulted in literally millions of new jobs in the eighties and nineties. The Reagan economic revolution was so successful and became so entrenched in the U.S. economy that multiple attempts to kill it didn't work."*

51

While we are on this topic of taxes, let us set the record straight once and for all on this subject. If anyone doubts that less government and lower taxes are the answer to healing a sick economy, let them study recent history after the Kennedy and Reagan tax cuts of the 1960s and 1980s. These were administrations represented by both of the two major American political parties. Unfortunately, the positive effects of the Kennedy tax cuts were short-lived thanks to L.B.J.'s massive spending on guns and butter (the Vietnam War and the explosion of welfare). While the Kennedy cuts were not nearly as dramatic as the Reagan tax cuts, they nevertheless were a big positive for the U.S. economy. The Reagan tax cuts were an altogether different story. They were much more aggressive and led to the largest and longest peacetime expansion of the American economy in U.S. history. "Reaganomics" worked so well that it resulted in literally millions of new jobs in the eighties and nineties. The Reagan economic revolution was so successful and became so entrenched in the U.S. economy that multiple attempts to kill it didn't work. George Bush's tax increases of 1990 couldn't stop it. Even the massive Clinton tax hikes of 1993 couldn't kill it. Reaganomics spawned the computer tech boom of the 1990s and ultimately brought about the fall of the Soviet Union's "evil empire," ending communism in most of the world. Reagan's pro-growth policies even led to the U.S. government's first balanced budget since 1957.

Ronald Reagan simply followed what our founding fathers said to do, which was to provide for a strong defense of the nation and to stay out of the way of the people by reducing regulations and taxes. This wasn't rocket science; it was just being true to *genuine American ideals*. This all makes you wonder why it is often so difficult for people to see the overwhelming evidence that is placed right before them. Many politicians and economists argued at the time that Reaganomics wouldn't work. Reagan's vice president, George H. W. Bush, even coined a phrase to describe it as "voodoo economics" when he ran against Reagan in the primaries in 1980. Obviously we now have the advantage of history, which has *proven that Ronald Reagan was absolutely right*.

Okay, so we have just eliminated the income tax, thereby reducing the revenue to the federal government by 40 to 45 percent. We shall now discuss the specific changes needed in order to reduce the size and scope of the federal government.

BOLD SOLUTIONS TO REDUCE THE SIZE AND SCOPE OF THE FEDERAL GOVERNMENT UNDER THE SECOND AMERICAN REVOLUTION

Federal Spending Before and After the Second American Revolution
Specific proposals for cuts in spending by the U.S. Federal Government

Spending Category	2009 Spending	Proposed Cuts	Proposed 2014 Budget*	Comments
Social Security	$650 Billion	$50 Billion	$600 Billion	Fraud/Administrative reductions.
Medicare	$400 Billion	$50 Billion	$350 Billion	Fraud/Administrative reductions.
Defense Department	$650 Billion	$130 Billion	$520 Billion	Overall spending reduced 20%.
Medicaid	$250 Billion	$ 250 Billion	$ -0-	Will not exist on a national level.
Welfare/ Unemployment	$350 Billion	$350 Billion	$ -0-	Will not exist on a national level.
Interest on the Debt	$250 Billion	$ 150 Billion	$ 100 Billion	This cost will slowly go to zero.
Agriculture	$20 Billion	$20 Billion	$ -0-	Eliminate Department entirely.
Education	$60 Billion	$60 Billion	$ -0-	Eliminate Department entirely.
Energy	$25 Billion	$25 Billion	$ -0-	Eliminate Department entirely.
Labor	$10 Billion	$10 Billion	$ -0-	Eliminate Department entirely.
Housing	$35 Billion	$ 35 Billion	$ -0-	Eliminate Department entirely.
"All Other" Spending	$ 400 Billion	$ 200 Billion	$ 200 Billion	50% minimum average** cuts
Totals	**$ 3.1 Trillion**	**$ 1.33 Trillion**	**$1.77 Trillion**	

(All figures above are rounded.)
* For purposes of our comparisons, the 2014 proposed budget figures are assumed to be in constant 2009 dollars.
** Some categories of spending under "all other" will be entirely eliminated. Remaining categories will be reduced to varying degrees, resulting in an average minimum 50 percent reduction in spending in the "all other" areas.

As I have stated throughout this book, *the second American Revolution* will not be about *"tinkering at the margins or nibbling at the edges"* of our national problems. We are left with no choice but to be *bold* and take very aggressive and decisive action in order to save our great nation. Based on our past and current path of fiscal irresponsibility (with deficit spending now accelerating totally out of control), the only choices that are available to ***"We the People"*** are the following:

1. Default on our debt
2. Inflate our way out of it by printing massive amounts of money, thereby totally destroying our currency
3. Dramatically reduce the size and scope of the federal government of the United States of America

> *"Inflation is the 'coward's way' out of honoring your obligations."*

Choice 1 is *not* an option. The government will not default on our debt because honoring our debt obligations is our only means of convincing China and others to continue to loan us money. Choice 2 has been the policy of the United States government ever since we went off the gold standard in 1933 and began to print a "fiat" currency that was not backed by gold. Inflation is the "coward's way" out of honoring your obligations. Our inflation has been relatively moderate up to this point in time (with the exception of the late 1970s and early 1980s); however, with our recent levels of spending and debt accumulation, the only way to keep up will be to accelerate the printing of money and dramatically increase the money supply. This will result in creating massive hyperinflation. This inflation will debase and destroy our currency. The consequences of choice 2 will be that our creditors will stop loaning us money. Choice 1 is not an option, and choice 2 will *very soon* become a non-option as well. Therefore, choice 3 is our only acceptable course of action if ***"We the People"*** choose to do the right thing and honor our obligations. It is also the *only* choice for us if ***"We the People"*** desire to save our nation and be true to our founders and forefathers.

> *"Bernie Madoff may have 'made off' with billions of dollars of other people's money, but Bernie Madoff looks like a two-bit swindler when compared to our elected leaders in the U.S. Congress."*

What we have clearly learned over an extended period of time is that elitist, career politicians are very definitely *not* the kind of people you want managing your affairs. They have operated Social Security as a gigantic Ponzi scheme for the past fifty years. There is no such thing as a Social Security "trust fund." Our elected leaders have spent all of the money that we have paid in Social Security taxes and, as a consequence, have *stolen* future retirement income from you and millions of other American citizens. Bernie Madoff may have "made off" with billions of dollars of other people's money, but Bernie Madoff looks like a two-bit swindler when compared to our elected leaders in the U.S. Congress. We now need to relieve them all of their duties and find suitable replacements. The process of replacing them began in earnest on November 2, 2010, and will be complete in November 2014 when the last group of the current U.S. Senators who are serving in office will be up for reelection. It is totally up to *"We the People"* as to whether we choose to repair our government or whether we allow our current bunch of corrupt elected leaders to finish ruining our great nation. For patriotic Americans, this choice is an easy one. Throw them out and take back our Republic!

> *"If one were to set out to create the most inefficient way of helping people in need, it would be to do it through the federal government ... "*

We will now review how the people and the states are to adjust to the above reductions in federal spending. Let us begin with welfare. If one were to set out to create the most inefficient way of helping people in need, it would be to do it through the federal government, where as much as 70 percent of welfare budgets get eaten up in waste and bureaucracy. On that basis, if *"We the People"* spend $600 billion on welfare and unemployment at the federal level each year, then families, churches, communities, and our local and state governments would only need to spend $180 billion on *direct* benefits to recipients in order to have the *same or better* results. Better yet, even if we allow for 20 percent of funds collected at a local level to be used for administration and a local bureaucracy, *"We the People"* will need to be taxed at half or less at a local level to accomplish these same or better results. This alone will provide for a 50 percent tax cut for *every* American! Don't forget, we will no longer be paying any federal income tax. This approach assumes that *"We the People"* will begin taking more responsibility for ourselves once the federal government gets out of the welfare business. It is my firm belief that not only *will we* begin taking more individual responsibility for ourselves but that *"We the People"* actually *want* to do so.

A personal story to illustrate this point ...

My business partner, Jim Rea, and I were in Boston, Massachusetts for meetings in June of 2009. We were at a Dunkin' Donuts shop downtown having a breakfast sandwich and a cup of coffee one morning before starting our day. While we were seated there, an elderly gentleman walked in front of the store just outside the picture window. The gentleman looked disheveled, his clothes were soiled, his hair unkempt, and he was clearly struggling to make his way along. He was likely homeless. The man slowly made his way to the front door of the store and repeatedly looked inside and paced back and forth in front of the donut shop. Jim got up and went outside to speak with the man. The man held out his hand, in which he held a nickel and a dime. Jim asked if he wanted something to eat. The man held forth his hand filled with the nickel and dime and nodded his head up and down, indicating that yes, he wanted something to eat. Jim invited the man into the store and asked him what he would like. The man asked for a breakfast sandwich and a cup of hot tea. Jim ordered the food for the man and proceeded down the line to pay the cashier. When Jim pulled out the money to pay for the man's food, the cashier said to him, "*No, don't worry about it; I will take care of it.*" Jim offered once more to pay. Again, the lady said, "*No, I've got it.*" The elderly homeless man and the lady cashier at Dunkin' Donuts were of entirely different races. This true story clearly demonstrates that *American* kindness, generosity, and goodwill are alive and well today!

> "*Our founders had ... the wisdom to know that caring for people out of the national treasury was not the way to help them and that it would lead to exactly what we have today—graft, corruption, and a bloated federal bureaucracy.*"

People feel better about themselves when they can be self-reliant. In the event people are unable to be self-reliant for reasons that are beyond their own control, their fellow citizens in their *local community* feel good when they are able to help these less-fortunate folks. In fact, they *want* to help. Once the cycle of poverty is broken, everyone will be much better off, and our national productivity will be greatly improved. Our founders had great compassion for the needy. However, they had the *wisdom* to know that caring for people out of the national treasury was not the way to help them and that it would lead to exactly what we have today—graft, corruption, and a bloated federal bureaucracy.

Our founders also knew that it was unfair, and many of them actually declared it un-American, to make these decisions on behalf of taxpayers. That explains why they didn't allow direct transfer payments to individual citizens in our Constitution. It is a crying shame that we have had to learn this lesson the hard way when we could have simply paid attention to what our founders and forefathers had to say on the matter. Rather than ending it abruptly, the plan will be to cut the federal welfare budget by a third each year for three years until it is entirely eliminated on the federal level. This will give adequate time for the people, their families, their churches, and their communities, as well as our local and state governments, to adjust and to absorb this responsibility.

> *"people fell off the welfare rolls in droves, became self-reliant, and began to feel much better about themselves. The success stories were legion."*

By the way, we also have the advantage of history on our side as a nation when it comes to proving the need to end welfare on a national basis. Even *if* providing transfer payments to individuals from the federal treasury were allowed under the U.S. Constitution, and please bear in mind that our U.S. Constitution in no way provides or allows for these transfer payments, the Personal Responsibility and Work Opportunity Reconciliation Act of 1996 proves that there is no reason to continue them. A Democratic president, Bill Clinton, and a Republican Congress proved that welfare payments from the federal government are not necessary when they undertook welfare reform in 1996. After this welfare reform act in 1996, people were required to go to work within two years of receiving benefits, and there was a lifetime cap of five years placed on benefits. In the aftermath, people fell off the welfare rolls in droves, became self-reliant, and began to feel much better about themselves. The success stories were legion.

All societies will have poor people in them, and this will be the case *regardless* of how much money government or *"We the People"* spend on those living in poverty. However, by providing for needy folks on a *local* level, and in a compassionate way, they will have a chance to become self-sufficient in a much shorter time due to accountability being available and manageable. This will break the perpetual and generational cycles of dependency that have plagued America since the very early days of the federal government's first attempts to help poor people. Thanks to President Clinton and the 104th Congress, we have now learned this national lesson.

"The federal government didn't have any involvement whatsoever in the education of our children during the first three-quarters of our existence as a nation, and yet our children were much better educated in those days than they are in our day."

The Department of Education should be among the first departments to be entirely eliminated in our reorganization of the federal government. This entire episode in our history as a nation has been nothing short of a national embarrassment. The federal government didn't have any involvement whatsoever in the education of our children during the first three-quarters of our existence as a nation, and yet our children were much better educated in *those* days than they are in *our* day. One hundred years ago, the quality of education was much better than it is today. Several years ago, my business partner George Huffman showed me the final exam book that his father Lloyd (a teacher) gave his students when they graduated from the eighth grade. That particular exam was given in May 1915, nearly one hundred years ago. George Huffman was born in 1920, and his father Lloyd was born in 1891. Below is a scanned image that includes a sampling of some questions from that exam.

Please take note that this exam was given on a *Saturday*. The exam required the *entire day* to complete,as there was a morning and an afternoon set of questions. Judging from the "Notice to Applicants" in the rules section at the beginning of the exam, there was no guarantee that anyone would pass the exam. Evidence of this is clear in question #11—*"How many years have you spent in the eighth grade?"* and in #12—*"If you graduate, will you attend high school? Where?"* Wow! Obviously the concept of providing "social" promotion had not been thought of a hundred years ago, for it was clear from these questions that some of the students were expected to be attending eighth grade for more than just one year.

It is also quite clear from this exam that Americans one hundred years ago were *extremely* serious about educating their children. I would submit that it would be a daunting challenge in today's America for any twelfth-grade student graduating from high school or perhaps even a college senior to pass this exam! These folks didn't need any federal guidance or assistance in order to educate children. It is abundantly clear from this example that *local* township trustees who lived in the *local* community and were therefore directly *accountable* to the parents of the students did just fine in educating children! Your author believes that this is precisely the type of public education system to which America needs to return.

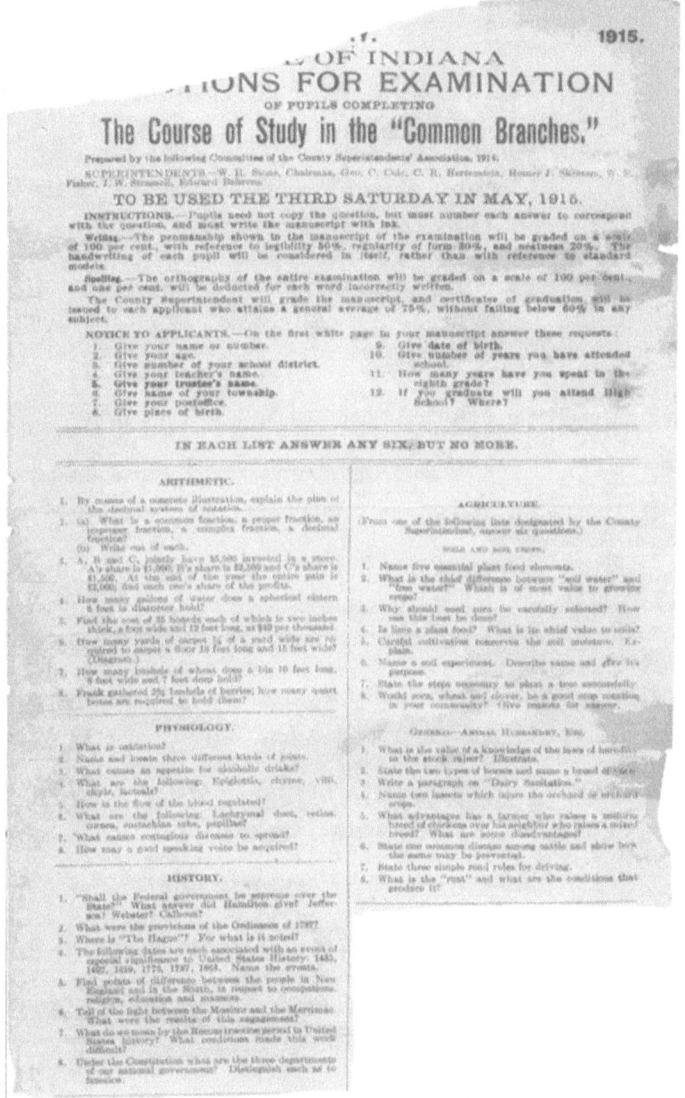

Now we know why an eighth-grade education was considered adequate in America one hundred years ago. These young folks were very adequately prepared to face the real world once they had mastered these subjects!

Below are some random test questions from the above Eighth Grade Exam:

Arithmetic: How many gallons of water does a spherical cistern six feet in diameter hold?

Physiology: What are the following: Lachrymal duct, retina, cornea, Eustachian tube, and papillae?

History: Shall the Federal Government be supreme over the State? What answer did Hamilton give? Jefferson? Webster? Calhoun?

Agriculture: Name five essential plant food elements.

Grammar: Compare and contrast the adjective and adverb, noun and pronoun, preposition and conjunction.

Geography: Name the kind of government found in each of the following countries: Germany, United States, Portugal, Japan, China, Brazil, Canada, France, Italy, Turkey

Reading: In the drama of *Julius Caesar*, are your sympathies with Caesar or his enemies? Why?

Industrial Arts: What is meant by joints in woodwork? Name two kinds of joints and tell how each is made.

Music: What is the use of Sharps? Flats?

Domestic Science: What is a simple test for fresh eggs?

Indiana History: Give an accounting of Abraham Lincoln's life in Indiana.

Civics: Why do we have courts? Why do we have legislatures?

Art: Make a pencil sketch suitable for use on an Easter card.

Cooking: What causes the spoiling of fruits, vegetables, and meals?

Household Management: Why should the mother and father be members of community organizations?

While we are on this subject of education, let's consider "homeschooling" for a moment. Over the past three decades, millions of Americans became fed up with the mediocrity of the public school system. As a result, parents began teaching their children at home. My brother Tim and his wife Annalynn have five children ranging from fifteen to twenty-eight years of age. Annalynn has homeschooled each of these children during the majority of their primary education years (grades kindergarten through twelfth). Below are the results of those efforts:

Danielle, the eldest, now twenty-eight, holds a bachelor's and a master's degree in occupational therapy.

Lauren, now twenty-six, holds a mechanical engineering degree from Notre Dame and a law degree from the University of Pittsburg. Lauren is a patent attorney.

Nicola, twenty-four, holds a chemical engineering degree from Notre Dame. Nicola is a chemical engineer with British Petroleum.

I believe the odds are excellent that the two younger ones, Thomas and James, will likewise flourish.

Could there be any possibility that their mother Annalynn's efforts on behalf of these children had a positive influence on the success of their outstanding educational outcome? While statistical proof might not be possible, I would pin my hopes and put my money on the efforts of Annalynn and millions of other parents just like her. It is important to note that most of our founding fathers were very highly educated men. Do you know what is also common about most of them? Most of them were to a great extent homeschooled. George Washington, father of our country, was homeschooled. Benjamin Franklin, the fifteenth of seventeen children and America's most celebrated inventor and thinker, was *entirely* homeschooled. Thomas Jefferson was afforded a formal education by virtue of his father leaving funds at his death (Jefferson's father died when Thomas was age fourteen) for the express purpose of educating him. Jefferson was known to study for fifteen hours per day. While he was not one of our founding fathers, Abraham Lincoln was almost entirely self-taught. Lincoln had an insatiable desire to learn, and this lasted throughout his entire life.

A prime example illustrating the mistake of making decisions about children's education from a remote place can be found right in my own backyard. In the 1960s, the state of Indiana made the less-than-brilliant decision to consolidate school districts so that they covered entire counties rather than townships. The result was that children spent much of their day on school buses (where they learned things that would have been better saved for an older age), were placed in classrooms with many more students in them than was conducive to a quality education and learning, and were treated more like numbers than people. This change also created an environment in which parents had greater difficulty being actively involved in their children's education. Incidents of drug use and teenage pregnancy skyrocketed. When schools were consolidated, much of the "sense of community" was forever lost in many small towns throughout America. I was a product of this Indiana school consolidation and can therefore attest that very little from Lloyd Huffman's "fundamental subjects" of 1915 above were taught in Indiana public schools in the 1960s and 1970s. I can tell you from firsthand experience that school consolidation turned out to be an overall unmitigated disaster for the quality of education in Indiana.

CHAPTER FIVE

TERM LIMITS FOR THE U.S. CONGRESS

FEBRUARY 27, 1951—A GOOD START

Twenty-Second (22nd) Amendment to the U.S. Constitution

"No person shall be elected to the office of the President more than twice, and no person who has held the office of President, or acted as President, for more than two years of a term to which some other person was elected President shall be elected to the office of the President more than once ... "

March 21, 1947—Presidential Term Limits was passed in the U.S. Congress.

February 27, 1951—Finally ratified by the states, the amendment became law.

"There was an entire generation of people ... who truly had come to believe the nation itself would come to an end now that President Roosevelt had died. This event was widely viewed as dangerous for our nation."

The Twenty-Second Amendment to the U.S. Constitution was passed by the U.S. Congress on March 21, 1947, and was ratified by enough states (75 percent) to become law on February 27, 1951. Franklin D. Roosevelt made the passage of the Twenty-Second Amendment necessary when he violated the long-held tradition of a two-term limit begun by our first president, George Washington, and honored by the next thirty presidents who followed Washington. Roosevelt campaigned for and won not one, not two, not three, but *four* terms to the U.S. presidency. Upon his death in 1945, it became immediately clear that we could never do this again. Thousands of young adults had grown up as children and passed well into adulthood never having known any president other than F.D.R. There was an entire generation of people at the time who truly had come to believe the nation itself would come to an end now that President Roosevelt had died. This event was widely viewed as dangerous for our nation. Thomas Jefferson wrote the following in 1807 regarding presidential term limits:

> *"If some termination to the services of the chief Magistrate be not fixed by the Constitution, or supplied by practice, his office, nominally four years, will in fact become for life..."*
>
> **—Thomas Jefferson** in 1807

Thomas Jefferson had no way to know that his prediction would literally become reality, for Roosevelt would die in office! Why didn't our founders address this in the U.S. Constitution? We may never have a clear answer to this question, but thankfully the founders did provide an avenue for us to amend the document—and so we did.

Thomas Jefferson not only respected and honored the tradition first set by George Washington to voluntarily limit the terms of the U.S. Presidency to just two; he also knew that we should limit the terms of Congress. In the statement below, Jefferson is clearly *not* limiting his comments to just the terms of the U.S. Presidency.

"To prevent every danger which might arise to American freedom from continuing too long in office, it is earnestly recommended that we set an obligation on the holder of that office to go out after a certain period."

—Thomas Jefferson

It seems that we have come full circle in the two hundred years between 1807 and 2012. Our nation's original Constitution did not provide for *any* form of term limits on any federal office. Despite this, our founders as well as the leaders who followed for the next more than a hundred years held to a tradition of *voluntarily* limiting their time in office. Then in the early part of the twentieth century, elected leaders began to ignore the tradition until Franklin D. Roosevelt's actions of seeking and winning four terms to the U.S. presidency resulted in the passage and the ratification of the Twenty-Second Amendment to the U.S. Constitution, which is shown and described above. **"We the People"** now need to force the same limitations on our other federal representatives in the U.S. Congress.

President Obama for Life?

(The above banner is taken from Rep. Serrano's Web site: www.serrano.house.gov.)

We now find ourselves at a very dangerous point in our history. A U.S. congressman from the state of New York has sponsored legislation that would repeal the Twenty-Second Amendment to the U.S. Constitution. This is scary stuff. Representative Jose Serrano on January 6, 2009, filed the following legislation in the Congress:

HJ 5 IH   111TH CONGRESS, 1ST SESSION
H.J. RES.

Proposing an amendment to the Constitution of the United States to repeal the Twenty-second atricle of amendment, thereby removing the limitation of the number of terms an individual may serve as president.

IN THE HOUSE OF REPRESENTATIVES
January 6, 2009

Mr. SERRANO introduced the following joint resolution; which was referred to the Committee on the Judiciary.

JOINT RESOLUTION

Proposing an amendment to the Constitution of the United States to repeal the Twenty-second article of amendment, thereby removing the limitation on the number of terms an individual may serve as President.

Resolved by the Senate and House of Representatives of the United States of America in Congress assembled (two-thirds of each House concurring therein), That the following article is proposed as an amendment to the Constitution of the United States, which shall be valid to all intents and purposes as part of the Constitution when ratified by the legislatures of three-fourths of the several States within seven years after the date of its submission for ratification:

ARTICLE—

'The Twenty-second article of amendment to the Constitution of the United States is hereby repealed.'

So there you have it—President Obama, or some future president, *for life.* Scary, isn't it? There is no need to panic quite yet. Amending the Constitution requires a two-thirds (2/3) majority vote in both houses of Congress to pass and then an additional hurdle of three-fourths (3/4) of the states to ratify it before the amendment can go into effect. Nevertheless, this is an ominous sign of the mentality of at least one so-called representative of the people who is currently leading our great nation. This action in early 2009 makes it all the more urgent that *"We the People"* act on requiring that a Term Limits Amendment be passed by Congress and ratified by the States. You will read at the end of this chapter that it is well within the power of *"We the People"* to accomplish this.

> *"Nothing so strongly impels a man to regard the interest of his constituents, as the certainty of returning to the general mass of the people from whence he was taken, where he must participate in their burdens."*
>
> —**George Mason** (1725–1792), in a June 17, 1788,
> Speech in the Virginia Ratifying Convention.

George Mason was a founding father and, along with James Madison, is considered the "Father of the Bill of Rights."

"All men having power ought to be mistrusted."

—James Madison,
fourth President of the United States of America, 1809–1817

"All power in human hands is liable to be abused."

—James Madison, December 18, 1825.
Considered by many to be the "Father of the Constitution."
Also considered by many to be the "Father of the Bill of Rights."

A New Push for a Term Limits Amendment to the U.S. Constitution

*"one could easily argue that the sum total of what we have
accomplished these past 250 years has been to simply replace
one set of foreign rulers in the form of a royal monarchy
on the far side of the Atlantic with a new set of domestic
rulers on the East Coast of our own homeland in the form
of a perpetual royal oligarchy."*

A Term Limits Amendment to the U.S. Constitution limiting
the number of terms in office that our U.S. House and Senate federal
representatives may serve is much needed and is long overdue. The effort

to bring about this change should not *and must not* be further delayed. Given the way in which we operate the U.S. government, one could easily argue that the sum total of what we have accomplished these past 250 years has been to simply replace one set of foreign rulers in the form of a royal monarchy on the far side of the Atlantic with a new set of domestic rulers on the East Coast of our own homeland in the form of a perpetual royal oligarchy. Our current career political system virtually guarantees that little to nothing of any real substance for the good of the nation will occur in government.

Not one of our elected officials will risk losing the next election if it means going out on a limb and proposing that we actually begin to behave rationally on fiscal issues or that we actually secure our borders. God forbid that we should actually begin observing the principles and intent of our founders by returning the Liberty and Freedom to the people that was to be guaranteed us under the U.S. Constitution. It should be no surprise that our national legislature can't get anything meaningful accomplished, for there are no "fresh ideas" to be found in Washington DC. The United States is plagued with corrupt, elitist, career politicians who are more interested in staying in power and lining their own pockets than in justly and honorably serving this great nation of ours. These politicians are more beholden to lobbyists and special interest groups than they are to the folks back home. We need to sweep them all from office and start over.

> *"Our goal should be to design the final result so that the system will attract only those Americans who are running for office to serve for the right reasons, those reasons being to selflessly serve their nation and their constituents back home."*

Most Americans agree that our current system of electing federal representatives is broken. The opinion of this farmer from Indiana (and by the way, it is also the opinion of more than 80 percent of the U.S. population) is that we desperately need to amend the Constitution of the United States to require that term limits be placed on people serving in the U.S. Congress. This is the only way that we can protect our elected officials from "themselves" by eliminating the desire to win an office solely for the dual purposes of personal financial gain and self-aggrandizement. Our goal should be to design the final result so that the system will attract *only* those Americans who are running for office to serve for the *right* reasons, those reasons being to selflessly serve their nation and their constituents back home. This is an essential step if we are going to be able to once and for all solve the serious problems that confront our nation. We need the involvement of *new people* with *fresh ideas*. With "term limits done right," we will once again enjoy the true *representative* government that our founders worked so hard to create for us instead of what we have evolved into, which is a "perpetual royal oligarchy" made up of the same tired group of people with their old, stale, and worn-out ideas. Unfortunately, in today's world, we do not have the same high caliber of people we had at the beginning of our nation's founding and up through Abraham Lincoln's time. People during those early days of our nation were willing to seek office for the noblest of reasons; that is sadly *not* the case today. Due to this societal change, term limits have now become a *necessity*.

As you read earlier in this book, Abraham Lincoln ran for the U.S. House of Representatives in 1846 and won a two-year term. At that time, there was an understanding that, if elected, a person would serve one term and then go home and back to work in the "real world." This was a long-standing tradition from the very beginning of our nation, and it made room for many others to serve their country. Despite the fact that he loved the job and would very likely have been reelected, Lincoln honored the long-held tradition of the time and did not even seek a second term. Unfortunately, as evidence of the past century has proven, a noble attitude like this by the politicians of today is just too much to expect in the reality of our current world. It is interesting to note that the sentiment of stepping aside and allowing others to serve actually reached its peak right at the time Lincoln served in the U.S. House of Representatives. See Figure 1 below to learn more about what has transpired over the course of our history as respects the reelection rates of members of the U.S. Congress.

Abraham Lincoln
Sixteenth President of the
United States of America
Born 1809—Died 1865

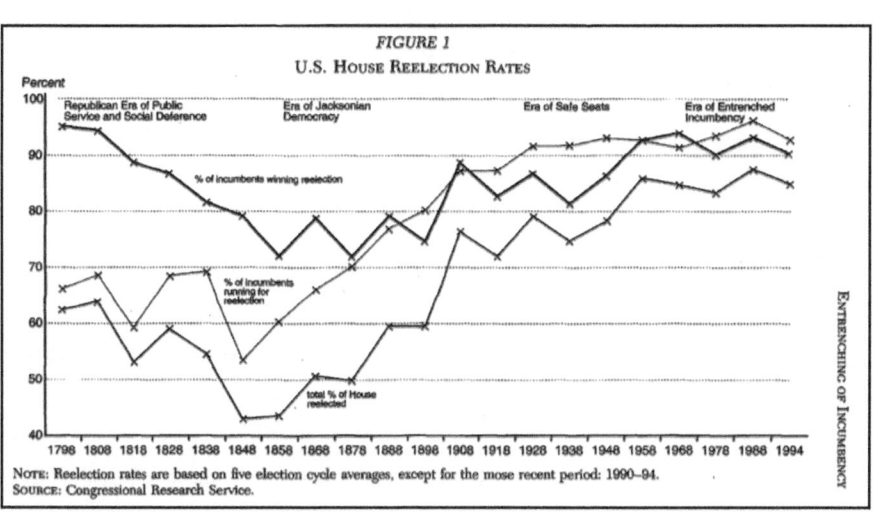

FIGURE 1
U.S. House Reelection Rates

NOTE: Reelection rates are based on five election cycle averages, except for the most recent period: 1990–94.
SOURCE: Congressional Research Service.

Some Interesting As Well As Disturbing Facts

1. In November 2004, of the 401 incumbent U.S. House members who sought reelection, *all* but *five* were reelected. That equates to a *99* percent reelection rate for members of the U.S. House of Representatives!

2. In November 2004, of the twenty-six incumbent U.S. Senate members who sought reelection, *all* but *one* were reelected. That equates to a *96* percent reelection rate for members of the U.S. Senate!

3. As of January 20, 2006, *over 40* percent of the members of the U.S. House and Senate had served for *more than thirty years.* That means *224* members of the U.S. Congress had held office for more than *thirty* years each!

4. In 2008, a candidate challenging an incumbent U.S. Senator was outspent by that incumbent by an average of over $7,500,000. A candidate challenging an incumbent U.S. House member was outspent by that incumbent by an average of over $1,000,000.

5. The current salary for the majority of the members of Congress is $174,000 per year to compensate them for their three-day workweek. This fact puts these people in the *top 5 percent* of all incomes in the United States.

6. The current salary for the Speaker of the House of Representatives is $223,500 per year.

7. The current salary for the President of the United States is $400,000 per year.

8. Lobbyists spend roughly an astounding *$5 million per member* of Congress each year to sway those members of Congress toward voting in favor of any number of the lobbyists' special interests.

9. *Each* member of the U.S. Congress has from fourteen to eighteen staff people and spends between $1.3 and $1.6 million each year just on expenses related to running their office.

10. The U.S. Congress voted themselves an additional $93,000 each in *petty cash* in January 2009!

11. On average, over the last nine years, Congress has met about 140 (39%) days during each calendar year.

> *"...why do politicians keep getting reelected at obscene rates of more than 95 percent? It is because they get to choose who votes for them."*

As to #1 and #2 above: If the politicians we are electing are financially driving our nation into the ground, why do they keep getting reelected at these obscene rates of more than 95 percent? It is because they get to choose who votes for them. It is called gerrymandering, a system that allows congressional districts to be redrawn at the whim of the politicians. Under this system, politicians essentially can pick and choose who they want to represent. As a result, congressional districts look more like a scribble on the map by a three-year-old than the neat and tidy blocks of districts that you and I would draw. The two aims of gerrymandering are to maximize the effect of supporters' votes and to minimize the effect of opponents' votes. It is done to favor incumbent politicians. While the federal government outlawed "redlining" (the practice of discriminating by geographic area) to avoid discrimination in the Fair Housing Act of 1968, the same people who passed that law don't seem to mind using discrimination when designing their congressional districts so that they can "segregate" people by racial minorities, ethnic groups, and so on when it is to their advantage in getting reelected. Did someone say hypocrite? See below (from Wikipedia.org) two examples of gerrymandered districts.

Printed in 1812, this political cartoon illustrates the electoral districts drawn by the Massachusetts legislature to favor the incumbent Democratic-Republican Party candidates of Governor Elbridge "Gerry" over the Federalists, from which the term gerrymander is derived. The cartoon depicts the bizarre shape of a district in Essex County, Massachusetts as a dragon. The painter, Gilbert Stuart, likened it to a salamander, and the editor, Benjamin Russel, advised "Better say a Gerrymander." The name stuck.

Congressional District 4

The earmuff shape of Illinois's 4th Congressional district connects two Hispanic neighborhoods, while remaining contiguous by narrowly tracing Interstate 294.

"What 'We the People' have is an aristocracy running our country."

As to #3 and #4 above: The U.S. Congress has *thirty* members who have been serving for more than *thirty years*, and there are a handful of them who have been there more than *forty years*! What ***"We the People"*** have is an *aristocracy* running our country. Is it any wonder that we don't have the new ideas that are needed to solve our nation's problems? Have you ever considered why we can't seem to get the caliber of people to run for office that we could really get excited about voting for—like honest, hardworking, patriotic people? Or maybe some businesspeople who are able to understand and repair our financial problems? It is because entrenched career, elitist politicians lock them out of the system! This must change. Term limits are the solution to this.

As to #5, #6, and #7 above: During the first 158 years of the United States, members of Congress received pay of around $1,000 per year in the very beginning, and it never exceeded $10,000 in those first 158 years. Over the past sixty years, compensation has rapidly grown to now $174,000 plus pensions and other special benefits. George Washington refused to accept *any* compensation whatsoever during the eight years that he served as commander in chief during the Revolutionary War. When the Constitution was adopted, it called for an annual salary for the President of $25,000. George Washington also refused the $25,000. Please understand that Washington didn't refuse the pay because it wasn't needed. Fighting the Revolution had left him in great need of money. Many of our founders considered it beneath their dignity to receive compensation of any kind to serve their nation. They felt it was their *duty* to serve, and many were offended if offered compensation. *Wow*, how times have changed.

As to #8, #9, #10, and #11 above: There are *insane* amounts of money sloshing around our elected leaders. It is no wonder politicians leave office as multimillionaires, no matter their station in life when they first took office. This all needs to be outlawed, and there is a very simple and unique way of accomplishing that goal. Details will follow at the end of this chapter under Solutions. Meanwhile, let's continue our term limits discussion.

> *"Society in every state is a blessing, but government, even in its best state, is but a necessary evil; in its worst state, an intolerable one."*
>
> —**Thomas Paine**, *Common Sense*, 1776

Some newly elected representatives can still see the forest despite the trees. Let's have some more new ones in 2012 and 2014!

> *"Today's federal government is too big, too powerful, and too expensive because it is doing things beyond the scope of the Constitution. This is foolish, and it is dangerous."*
>
> —**Dr. Paul Broun**,
> newly elected in 2007 as a U.S. House Representative from Georgia

What Form Should Term Limits Take?

"Because more than 80 percent of the American people are now in favor of term limits, we most assuredly know that we should have them."

There are many ways to argue what *form* term limits should take, and there are a multitude of combinations that might be appropriate. However, there is only *one* decision to make when considering *whether* or not we need them. That decision is answered by a simple *yes* or no. Because more than 80 percent of the American people are now in favor of term limits, we most assuredly know that we should have them. Therefore, perhaps it is really of no great concern what final form term limits will take. It may be likely that most reasonable people would agree that no one person should be allowed to serve longer than twelve years in any federal office. If that is agreed to, the final form the amendment takes is really unimportant. The important thing is that we pass the Constitutional Amendment, and it finally appears that our country is now ready for that action.

"Once anyone has served two terms in one national office, they should not be allowed to run for any other office, except perhaps if we have a real statesman on our hands and that person desires to compete for the presidency."

What form do you believe term limits should take? Do we limit the U.S. Congress to two terms for both the House and Senate (totaling four years for the House and twelve for the Senate), just like the presidency? Do we go with eight years total to match the limit of the President's years in office by changing both the Senate and House terms to four years? Perhaps we should just change the House terms to four years. This would allow elected officials more time to get things done and not exhaust the candidates with nonstop election cycles. Terms could be rotated so that we continue our two-year election cycle. This would also allow us to provide for the constant flow of fresh ideas that we so desperately need. It also seems reasonable and prudent that candidates not be allowed to run for any *new* office while they are serving in their *current* one. Too much time is wasted on the campaign trail. The result is that the elected officials are not "serving" in their current office. This really creates a form of "theft" from the American people. Once anyone has served two terms in one national office, they should not be allowed to run for any other office, except perhaps if *"We the People"* have a real statesman on our hands and that person desires to compete for the presidency.

WE'VE BEEN HERE BEFORE

"our elected officials of today do not have the courage to vote themselves out of office. 'We the People' are therefore left with no option but to do it for them."

In 1994, the Republican Party ran on a platform during the midterm elections called the "Contract with America." Their "contract" detailed ten specific action items that Congress would undertake if the election resulted in a Republican Party victory large enough to wrest control away from the Democrats. Included among those ten items was an amendment to the U.S. Constitution that would have imposed twelve-year term limits on members of the U.S. Congress (i.e., six terms for Representatives, two terms for Senators). It was passed by the U.S. House in a 227–204 vote but failed to meet the Constitutional Amendment requirement of a two-thirds majority (instead of a simple majority). The measure therefore went down in defeat. What we learned from this experience is that when it comes right down to it, *our elected officials of today do not have the courage to vote themselves out of office.* *"We the People"* are therefore left with no option but to do it for them.

"Experience should teach us to be most on our guard to protect liberty when the government's purposes are beneficent... the greatest dangers to liberty lurk in insidious encroachment by men of zeal, well-meaning but without understanding."

—Justice Louis Brandeis, 1856–1941,
who served as Justice to the U.S. Supreme Court
from 1916 to 1939

Keep in mind that it is not easy to amend the Constitution of the United States and the process takes time. In many cases, five years or more have gone by between the time that an amendment is passed by Congress and ultimately ratified by the required number of states. The founders purposely made it difficult to amend the U.S. Constitution. They did not want our Constitution to be easily changed at the whim of a simple majority of legislators. The founders required a two-thirds (2/3) majority of the U.S. Congress to agree to any change in the Constitution. Once that hurdle is met, three-fourths (3/4) of the states have to vote in favor of the act of Congress in order to ratify the amendment. The founders wanted to make certain that there was an overwhelming need for a change and that a great majority of the people were in favor of such a change. So, if our current U.S. House and U.S. Senate officials are unwilling to do the right thing in passing a Term Limits Amendment to the U.S. Constitution, this begs the question: *How are we ever going to be able to accomplish the task?* It seems that we are in a sort of "Catch-22." The solution is really quite simple and can actually be accomplished in the 2012 and 2014 election cycles. All that is required is that *"We the People"* simply need to elect enough new members to Congress who are willing to make the change. And just how do we accomplish that feat? Next is where we begin to offer the solutions.

SOLUTION TO AMENDING THE U.S. CONSTITUTION BY PUTTING IN PLACE TERM LIMITS FOR THE CONGRESS

"Voters should vote only for a candidate … who is in favor of and pledges to support a Term Limits Amendment."

Prior to the 2012 and 2014 elections, a grassroots movement must encourage all of the electorate in the United States to vote *only* for candidates who are *new* to office *and* who are willing to commit to vote in favor of a Term Limits Amendment to the Constitution. We have two opportunities in 2012 and 2014 to make this happen. Voters should vote *only* for a candidate who is in favor of and pledges to support a Term Limits Amendment. Of necessity, this will require voting against *all* incumbents. We must vote the current officeholder (incumbent) out of office, as they have demonstrated in the recent past their unwillingness to pass such an amendment. It will take a concerted effort by a large percentage of voting Americans, but it can be done. In fact, it must be done if we are to honor the sacrifices of our founders by restoring true representative government.

SOLUTIONS TO BRINGING A COMPETITIVE ENVIRONMENT AND ETHICS TO THE ELECTION PROCESS

"It is the firm belief of your author that… American patriots are out there, just waiting for an opportunity to help restore the principles and values of our founding fathers."

Once *"We the People"* have elected a new "people's" Congress, they will then have a mandate to:

1. Pass a Term Limits Amendment to the U.S. Constitution and send it to the States for ratification.

2. Reset the Congressional districts on a simple and fair basis and outlaw gerrymandering forever.

3. Outlaw lobbying entirely and, along with it, fundraising by political candidates or political parties. This will create a level playing field for all candidates who wish to run for elective office. The public will finance all campaigns out of the treasury for Congress and the Presidency. Debates will be held on public television during a series of evenings, and candidates can make their case.

4. Do a top-to-bottom review of compensation for the Congress, how much time they spend in their home districts, the size of their staffs, their budgets, and so on. Certainly an end should be made to any pensions for members of Congress, as it will be unlawful for them to serve for a length of time that would entitle them to any retirement benefits. Besides, the goal is to attract *"citizen"* statesmen who desire to serve their country out of a sense of duty, and not out of any motivation involving financial gain. We are changing the emphasis. In this way, we will attract an entirely "new and different" public servant than we have in the recent past. As we "elevate the process," we will begin to attract true patriots, people who up to this point have been unwilling to step forward due to their high ethical standards and refusal to compromise their long-held values. It is my firm belief these American patriots are out there, just waiting for an opportunity to help restore the principles and values of our founding fathers.

5. Begin the immediate elimination of many federal departments and their programs, as well as begin dismantling the federal welfare state, evolving it back to individuals, families, local, and state governments. Begin selling off and liquidating much of the valuable real estate held by the U.S. federal government and use the sale proceeds to pay down the U.S. national debt.

6. Pass amendments to the U.S. Constitution for a balanced budget and a presidential line item veto. Having narrowly escaped a financial Armageddon that would have led to the very demise of our great nation, we now need an abundance of caution to make certain that we never again face the same risks to our nation's future. Requiring a balanced budget by the federal government will provide the security we need going

forward. The only exception to this amendment will be in the event of war. Only Congress is empowered to declare war. And no more passing the buck to the President! A presidential line item veto will work hand in glove with the balanced budget.

7. Amend the Constitution to limit Supreme Court Justices and other federal judges to a nine-year term, requiring that, at a minimum, they are reconfirmed each nine years.

DECLARATION OF INDEPENDENCE

Here is the complete text of the Declaration of Independence.
The original spelling and capitalization have been retained.
(Adopted by Congress on July 4, 1776)

THE UNANIMOUS DECLARATION OF THE
THIRTEEN UNITED STATES OF AMERICA

When, in the course of human events, it becomes necessary for one people
to dissolve the political bonds which have connected them with another,
and to assume among the powers of the earth, the separate and equal
station to which the laws of nature and of nature's God entitle them, a
decent respect to the opinions of mankind requires that they should declare
the causes which impel them to the separation.

We hold these truths to be self-evident, that all men are created equal,
that they are endowed by their Creator with certain unalienable rights,
that among these are life, Liberty and the pursuit of happiness. That to
secure these rights, governments are instituted among men, deriving their
just powers from the consent of the governed, that whenever any form
of government becomes destructive to these ends, it is the right of the
people to alter or to abolish it, and to institute new government, laying
its foundation on such principles, and organizing its powers in such form,
as to them shall seem most likely to effect their safety and happiness.
Prudence, indeed, will dictate that governments long established should not
be changed for light and transient causes; and accordingly all experience
hath shown that mankind are more disposed to suffer, while evils are
sufferable, than to right themselves by abolishing the forms to which they
are accustomed. But when a long train of abuses and usurpations, pursuing
invariably the same object, evinces a design to reduce them under absolute
despotism, it is their right, it is their duty, to throw off such government,
and to provide new guards for their future security. —Such has been the
patient sufferance of these colonies; and such is now the necessity which
constrains them to alter their former systems of government. The history
of the present King of Great Britain is a history of repeated injuries and
usurpations, all having in direct object the establishment of an absolute
tyranny over these states. To prove this, let facts be
submitted to a candid world.

He has refused his assent to laws, the most wholesome and necessary
for the public good.

He has forbidden his governors to pass laws of immediate and pressing
importance, unless suspended in their operation till his assent should be
obtained; and when so suspended, he has utterly neglected
to attend to them.

He has refused to pass other laws for the accommodation of large districts
of people, unless those people would relinquish the right of representation
in the legislature, a right inestimable to them and formidable
to tyrants only.

He has called together legislative bodies at places unusual, uncomfortable,
and distant from the depository of their public records, for the sole purpose
of fatiguing them into compliance with his measures.

He has dissolved representative houses repeatedly, for opposing with manly
firmness his invasions on the rights of the people.

He has refused for a long time, after such dissolutions, to cause others to
be elected; whereby the legislative powers, incapable of annihilation, have
returned to the people at large for their exercise; the state remaining in the
meantime exposed to all the dangers of invasion from without,
and convulsions within.

He has endeavored to prevent the population of these states; for that
purpose obstructing the laws for naturalization of foreigners; refusing to
pass others to encourage their migration hither, and raising the conditions
of new appropriations of lands.

He has obstructed the administration of justice, by refusing his assent to
laws for establishing judiciary powers.

He has made judges dependent on his will alone, for the tenure of their
offices, and the amount and payment of their salaries.

He has erected a multitude of new offices, and sent hither swarms of officers
to harass our people, and eat out their substance.

He has kept among us, in times of peace, standing armies without the
consent of our legislature.

He has affected to render the military independent of and
superior to civil power.

He has combined with others to subject us to a jurisdiction foreign to our
constitution, and unacknowledged by our laws; giving his assent to their
acts of pretended legislation:

For quartering large bodies of armed troops among us:

For protecting them, by mock trial, from punishment for any murders
which they should commit on the inhabitants of these states:

For cutting off our trade with all parts of the world:

For imposing taxes on us without our consent:

For depriving us in many cases, of the benefits of trial by jury:

For transporting us beyond seas to be tried for pretended offenses:

For abolishing the free system of English laws in a neighboring province, establishing therein an arbitrary government, and enlarging its boundaries so as to render it at once an example and fit instrument for introducing the same absolute rule in these colonies:

For taking away our charters, abolishing our most valuable laws, and altering fundamentally the forms of our governments:

For suspending our own legislatures, and declaring themselves invested with power to legislate for us in all cases whatsoever.

He has abdicated government here, by declaring us out of his protection and waging war against us.

He has plundered our seas, ravaged our coasts, burned our towns, and destroyed the lives of our people.

He is at this time transporting large armies of foreign mercenaries to complete the works of death, desolation and tyranny, already begun with circumstances of cruelty and perfidy scarcely paralleled in the most barbarous ages, and totally unworthy the head of a civilized nation.

He has constrained our fellow citizens taken captive on the high seas to bear arms against their country, to become the executioners of their friends and brethren, or to fall themselves by their hands.

He has excited domestic insurrections amongst us, and has endeavored to bring on the inhabitants of our frontiers, the merciless Indian savages, whose known rule of warfare, is undistinguished destruction of all ages, sexes and conditions.

In every stage of these oppressions we have petitioned for redress in the most humble terms: our repeated petitions have been answered only by repeated injury. A prince, whose character is thus marked by every act which may define a tyrant, is unfit to be the ruler of a free people.

Nor have we been wanting in attention to our British brethren. We have warned them from time to time of attempts by their legislature to extend an unwarrantable jurisdiction over us. We have reminded them of the circumstances of our emigration and settlement here. We have appealed to their native justice and magnanimity, and we have conjured them by the ties of our common kindred to disavow these usurpations, which would inevitably interrupt our connections and correspondence. They too have been deaf to the voice of justice and of consanguinity. We must, therefore, acquiesce in the necessity, which denounces our separation, and hold them, as we hold the rest of mankind, enemies in war, in peace friends.

We, therefore, the representatives of the United States of America, in General Congress, assembled, appealing to the Supreme Judge of the world for the rectitude of our intentions, do, in the name, and by the authority of the good people of these colonies, solemnly publish and declare, that these united colonies are, and of right ought to be free and independent states; that they are absolved from all allegiance to the British Crown, and that all political connection between them and the state of Great Britain, is and ought to be totally dissolved; and that as free and independent states, they have full power to levy war, conclude peace, contract alliances, establish commerce, and to do all other acts and things which independent states may of right do. And for the support of this declaration, with a firm reliance on the protection of Divine Providence, we mutually pledge to each other our lives, our fortunes and our sacred honor.

New Hampshire: Josiah Bartlett, William Whipple, Matthew Thornton
Massachusetts: John Hancock, Samual Adams, John Adams,
Robert Treat Paine, Elbridge Gerry
Rhode Island: Stephen Hopkins, William Ellery
Connecticut: Roger Sherman, Samuel Huntington,
William Williams, Oliver Wolcott
New York: William Floyd, Philip Livingston, Francis Lewis, Lewis Morris
New Jersey: Richard Stockton, John Witherspoon, Francis Hopkinson,
John Hart, Abraham Clark
Pennsylvania: Robert Morris, Benjamin Rush, Benjamin Franklin, John
Morton, George Clymer, James Smith, George Taylor, James Wilson,
George Ross
Delaware: Caesar Rodney, George Read, Thomas McKean
Maryland: Samuel Chase, William Paca, Thomas Stone,
Charles Carroll of Carrollton
Virginia: George Wythe, Richard Henry Lee, Thomas Jefferson,
Benjamin Harrison, Thomas Nelson, Jr., Francis Lightfoot Lee,
Carter Braxton
North Carolina: William Hooper, Joseph Hewes, John Penn
South Carolina: Edward Rutledge, Thomas Heyward, Jr.,
Thomas Lynch, Jr., Arthur Middleton
Georgia: Button Gwinnett, Lyman Hall, George Walton

Source: The Pennsylvania Packet, July 8, 1776

The Constitution of the United States

Here is the complete text of the U.S. Constitution. The original spelling and capitalization have been retained.

We the People of the United States, in Order to form a more perfect Union, establish Justice, insure domestic Tranquility, provide for the common defence, promote the general Welfare, and secure the Blessings of Liberty to ourselves and our Posterity, do ordain and establish this Constitution for the United States of America.

Article I

Section 1. All legislative Powers herein granted shall be vested in a Congress of the United States, which shall consist of a Senate and House of Representatives.

Section 2. The House of Representatives shall be composed of Members chosen every second Year by the People of the several States, and the Electors in each State shall have the Qualifications requisite for Electors of the most numerous Branch of the State Legislature.

No Person shall be a Representative who shall not have attained to the age of twenty five Years, and been seven Years a Citizen of the United States, and who shall not, when elected, be an Inhabitant of that State in which he shall be chosen.

Representatives and direct Taxes shall be apportioned among the several States which may be included within this Union, according to their respective Numbers, which shall be determined by adding to the whole Number of free Persons, including those bound to Service for a Term of Years, and excluding Indians not taxed, three fifths of all other Persons. The actual Enumeration shall be made within three Years after the first Meeting of the Congress of the United States, and within every subsequent Term of ten Years, in such Manner as they shall by Law direct. The Number of Representatives shall not exceed one for every thirty Thousand, but each State shall have at Least one Representative; and until such enumeration shall be made, the State of New Hampshire shall be entitled to chuse three, Massachusetts eight, Rhode-Island and Providence Plantations one, Connecticut five, New-York six, New Jersey four, Pennsylvania eight, Delaware one, Maryland six, Virginia ten, North Carolina five, South Carolina five, and Georgia three.

When vacancies happen in the Representation from any State, the Executive Authority thereof shall issue Writs of Election to fill such Vacancies.

The House of Representatives shall chuse their Speaker and other Officers; and shall have the sole Power of Impeachment.

Section 3. The Senate of the United States shall be composed of two Senators from each State, chosen by the Legislature thereof, for six Years; and each Senator shall have one Vote.

Immediately after they shall be assembled in Consequence of the first Election, they shall be divided as equally as may be into three Classes. The Seats of the Senators of the first Class shall be vacated at the Expiration of the second Year, of the second Class at the Expiration of the fourth Year, and the third Class at the Expiration of the sixth Year, so that one third may be chosen every second Year; and if Vacancies happen by Resignation, or otherwise, during the Recess of the Legislature of any State, the Executive thereof may make temporary Appointments until the next Meeting of the Legislature, which shall then fill such Vacancies.

No Person shall be a Senator who shall not have attained to the Age of thirty Years, and been nine Years a Citizen of the United States and who shall not, when elected, be an Inhabitant of that State for which he shall be chosen.

The Vice President of the United States shall be president of the Senate, but shall have no Vote, unless they be equally divided.

The Senate shall chuse their other Officers, and also a president pro tempore, in the Absence of the Vice President, or when he shall exercise the Office of president of the United States.

The Senate shall have the sole Power to try all Impeachments. When sitting for that Purpose, they shall be on Oath or Affirmation. When the president of the United States is tried, the Chief Justice shall preside: And no Person shall be convicted without the Concurrence of two thirds of the Members present.

Judgment in Cases of Impeachment shall not extend further than to removal from Office, and disqualification to hold and enjoy any Office of Honor, Trust or Profit under the United States: but the Party convicted shall nevertheless be liable and subject to Indictment, Trial, Judgment and Punishment, according to Law.

Section 4. The Times, Places and Manner of holding Elections for Senators and Representatives, shall be prescribed in each State by the Legislature thereof;

but the Congress may at any time by Law make or alter such Regulations, except as to the Places of chusing Senators.

The Congress shall assemble at least once in every Year, and such Meeting shall be on the first Monday in December, unless they shall by Law appoint a different Day.

Section 5. Each House shall be the Judge of the Elections, Returns and Qualifications of its own Members, and a Majority of each shall constitute a Quorum to do Business; but a smaller Number may adjourn from day to day, and may be authorized to compel the Attendance of absent Members, in such Manner, and under such Penalties as each House may provide.

Each House may determine the Rules of its Proceedings, punish its Members for disorderly Behaviour, and, with the Concurrence of two thirds, expel a Member.

Each House shall keep a Journal of its Proceedings, and from time to time publish the same, excepting such Parts as may in their Judgment require Secrecy; and the Yeas and Nays of the Members of either House on any question shall, at the Desire of one fifth of those Present, be entered on the Journal.

Neither House, during the Session of Congress, shall, without the Consent of the other, adjourn for more than three days, nor to any other Place than that in which the two Houses shall be sitting.

Section 6. The Senators and Representatives shall receive a Compensation for their Services, to be ascertained by Law, and paid out of the Treasury of the United States. They shall in all Cases, except Treason, Felony and Breach of the Peace, be privileged from Arrest during their Attendance at the Session of their respective Houses, and in going to and returning from the same; and for any Speech or Debate in either House, they shall not be questioned in any other Place.

No Senator or Representative shall, during the Time for which he was elected, be appointed to any civil Office under the Authority of the United States, which shall have been created, or the Emoluments whereof shall have been encreased during such time: and no Person holding any Office under the United States, shall be a Member of either House during his Continuance in Office.

Section 7. All Bills for raising Revenue shall originate in the House of Representatives; but the Senate may propose or concur with Amendments as on other Bills.

Every Bill which shall have passed the House of Representatives and the Senate, shall, before it become a Law, be presented to the president of the United States; if he approve he shall sign it, but if not he shall return it, with his Objections to that House in which it shall have originated, who shall enter the Objections at large on their Journal, and proceed to reconsider it. If after such Reconsideration two thirds of that House shall agree to pass the Bill, it shall be sent, together with the Objections, to the other House, by which it shall likewise be reconsidered, and if approved by two thirds of that House, it shall become a Law. But in all such Cases the Votes of both Houses shall be determined by Yeas and Nays, and the Names of the Persons voting for and against the Bill shall be entered on the Journal of each House respectively. If any Bill shall not be returned by the president within ten Days (Sundays excepted) after it shall have been presented to him, the Same shall be a Law, in like Manner as if he had signed it, unless the Congress by their Adjournment prevent its Return, in which Case it shall not be a Law.

Every Order, Resolution, or Vote to which the Concurrence of the Senate and House of Representatives may be necessary (except on a question of Adjournment) shall be presented to the president of the United States; and before the Same shall take Effect, shall be approved by him, or being disapproved by him, shall be repassed by two thirds of the Senate and House of Representatives, according to the Rules and Limitations prescribed in the Case of a Bill.

Section 8. The Congress shall have Power To lay and collect Taxes, Duties, Imposts and Excises, to pay the Debts and provide for the common Defence and general Welfare of the United States; but all Duties, Imposts and Excises shall be uniform throughout the United States;

To borrow Money on the credit of the United States;

To regulate Commerce with foreign Nations, and among the several States, and with the Indian Tribes;

To establish an uniform Rule of Naturalization, and uniform Laws on the subject of Bankruptcies throughout the United States;

To coin Money, regulate the Value thereof, and of foreign Coin, and fix the Standard of Weights and Measures;

To provide for the Punishment of counterfeiting the Securities and current Coin of the United States;

To establish Post Offices and post Roads;

To promote the Progress of Science and useful Arts, by securing for limited Times to Authors and Inventors the exclusive Right to their respective Writings and Discoveries;

To constitute Tribunals inferior to the Supreme Court;

To define and punish Piracies and Felonies committed on the high Seas, and Offences against the Law of Nations;

To declare War, grant Letters of Marque and Reprisal, and make Rules concerning Captures on Land and Water;

To raise and support Armies, but no Appropriation of Money to that Use shall be for a longer Term than two Years;

To provide and maintain a Navy;

To make Rules for the Government and Regulation of the land and naval Forces;

To provide for calling forth the Militia to execute the Laws of the Union, suppress Insurrections and repel Invasions;

To provide for organizing, arming, and disciplining, the Militia, and for governing such Part of them as may be employed in the Service of the United States, reserving to the States respectively, the Appointment of the Officers, and the Authority of training the Militia according to the discipline prescribed by Congress;

To exercise exclusive Legislation in all Cases whatsoever, over such District (not exceeding ten Miles square) as may, by Cession of particular States, and the Acceptance of Congress, become the Seat of the Government of the United States, and to exercise like Authority over all Places purchased by the Consent of the Legislature of the State in which the Same shall be, for the Erection of Forts, Magazines, Arsenals, dock-Yards, and other needful Buildings;—And

To make all Laws which shall be necessary and proper for carrying into Execution the foregoing Powers, and all other Powers vested by this

Constitution in the Government of the United States, or in any Department or Officer thereof.

Section 9. The Migration or Importation of such Persons as any of the States now existing shall think proper to admit, shall not be prohibited by the Congress prior to the Year one thousand eight hundred and eight, but a Tax or duty may be imposed on such Importation, not exceeding ten dollars for each Person.

The Privilege of the Writ of Habeas Corpus shall not be suspended, unless when in Cases of Rebellion or Invasion the public Safety may require it.

No Bill of Attainder or ex post facto Law shall be passed.

No Capitation, or other direct, Tax shall be laid, unless in Proportion to the Census or Enumeration herein before directed to be taken.

No Tax or Duty shall be laid on Articles exported from any State.

No Preference shall be given by any Regulation of Commerce or Revenue to the Ports of one State over those of another: nor shall Vessels bound to, or from, one State, be obliged to enter, clear or pay Duties in another.

No Money shall be drawn from the Treasury, but in Consequence of Appropriations made by Law; and a regular Statement and Account of Receipts and Expenditures of all public Money shall be published from time to time.

No Title of Nobility shall be granted by the United States: And no Person holding any Office of Profit or Trust under them, shall, without the Consent of the Congress, accept of any present, Emolument, Office, or Title, of any kind whatever, from any King, Prince, or foreign State.

Section 10. No State shall enter into any Treaty, Alliance, or Confederation; grant Letters of Marque and Reprisal; coin Money; emit Bills of Credit; make any Thing but gold and silver Coin a Tender in Payment of Debts; pass any Bill of Attainder, ex post facto Law, or Law impairing the Obligation of Contracts, or grant any Title of Nobility.

No State shall, without the Consent of the Congress, lay any Imposts or Duties on Imports or Exports, except what may be absolutely necessary for executing its inspection Laws: and the net Produce of all Duties and Imposts, laid by any State on Imports or Exports, shall be for the Use of the Treasury of the United States; and all such Laws shall be subject to the Revision and Controul of the Congress.

No State shall, without the Consent of Congress, lay any Duty of Tonnage, keep Troops, or Ships of War in time of Peace, enter into any Agreement or Compact with another State, or with a foreign Power, or engage in War, unless actually invaded, or in such imminent Danger as will not admit of delay.

Article II

Section 1. The executive Power shall be vested in a president of the United States of America. He shall hold his Office during the Term of four Years, and, together with the Vice President, chosen for the same Term, be elected, as follows:

Each State shall appoint, in such Manner as the Legislature thereof may direct, a Number of Electors, equal to the whole Number of Senators and Representatives to which the State may be entitled in the Congress: but no Senator or Representative, or Person holding an Office of Trust or Profit under the United States, shall be appointed an Elector.

The Electors shall meet in their respective States, and vote by Ballot for two Persons, of whom one at least shall not be an Inhabitant of the same State with themselves. And they shall make a List of all the Persons voted for, and of the Number of Votes for each; which List they shall sign and certify, and transmit sealed to the Seat of the Government of the United States, directed to the president of the Senate. The president of the Senate shall, in the Presence of the Senate and House of Representatives, open all the Certificates, and the Votes shall then be counted. The Person having the greatest Number of Votes shall be the president, if such Number be a Majority of the whole Number of Electors appointed; and if there be more than one who have such Majority, and have an equal Number of Votes, then the House of Representatives shall immediately chuse by Ballot one of them for president; and if no Person have a Majority, then from the five highest on the List the said House shall in like Manner chuse the President. But in chusing the President, the Votes shall be taken by States, the Representation from each State having one Vote; A quorum for this Purpose shall consist of a Member or Members from two thirds of the States, and a Majority of all the States shall be necessary to a Choice. In every Case, after the Choice of the President, the Person having the greatest Number of Votes of the Electors shall be the Vice President. But if there should remain two or more who have equal Votes, the Senate shall chuse from them by Ballot the Vice President.

The Congress may determine the Time of chusing the Electors, and the Day on which they shall give their Votes; which Day shall be the same throughout the United States.

No Person except a natural born Citizen, or a Citizen of the United States, at the time of the Adoption of this Constitution, shall be eligible to the Office of President; neither shall any Person be eligible to that Office who shall not have attained to the Age of thirty five Years, and been fourteen Years a Resident within the United States.

In Case of the Removal of the President from Office, or of his Death, Resignation, or Inability to discharge the Powers and Duties of the said Office, the Same shall devolve on the Vice President, and the Congress may by Law provide for the Case of Removal, Death, Resignation or Inability, both of the President and Vice President, declaring what Officer shall then act as President, and such Officer shall act accordingly, until the Disability be removed, or a President shall be elected.

The President shall, at stated Times, receive for his Services, a Compensation, which shall neither be encreased nor diminished during the Period for which he shall have been elected, and he shall not receive within that Period any other Emolument from the United States, or any of them.

Before he enter on the Execution of his Office, he shall take the following Oath or Affirmation:—"I do solemnly swear (or affirm) that I will faithfully execute the Office of President of the United States, and will to the best of my Ability, preserve, protect and defend the Constitution of the United States."

Section 2. The President shall be Commander in Chief of the Army and Navy of the United States, and of the Militia of the several States, when called into the actual Service of the United States; he may require the Opinion, in writing, of the principal Officer in each of the executive Departments, upon any Subject relating to the Duties of their respective Offices, and he shall have Power to grant Reprieves and Pardons for Offences against the United States, except in Cases of Impeachment.

He shall have Power, by and with the Advice and Consent of the Senate, to make Treaties, provided two thirds of the Senators present concur; and he shall nominate, and by and with the Advice and Consent of the Senate, shall appoint Ambassadors, other public Ministers and Consuls, Judges of the supreme Court, and all other Officers of the United States, whose Appointments are not herein otherwise provided for, and which shall be established by Law: but the Congress may by Law vest the Appointment of such inferior Officers, as they think proper, in the President alone, in the Courts of Law, or in the Heads of Departments.

The President shall have Power to fill up all Vacancies that may happen during the Recess of the Senate, by granting Commissions which shall expire at the End of their next Session.

Section 3. He shall from time to time give to the Congress Information of the State of the Union, and recommend to their Consideration such Measures as he shall judge necessary and expedient; he may, on extraordinary Occasions, convene both Houses, or either of them, and in Case of Disagreement between them, with Respect to the Time of Adjournment, he may adjourn them to such Time as he shall think proper; he shall receive Ambassadors and other public Ministers; he shall take Care that the Laws be faithfully executed, and shall Commission all the Officers of the United States.

Section 4. The President, Vice President and all civil Officers of the United States, shall be removed from Office on Impeachment for, and Conviction of, Treason, Bribery, or other high Crimes and Misdemeanors.

Article III

Section 1. The judicial Power of the United States, shall be vested in one supreme Court, and in such inferior Courts as the Congress may from time to time ordain and establish. The Judges, both of the supreme and inferior Courts, shall hold their Offices during good Behaviour, and shall, at stated Times, receive for their Services, a Compensation, which shall not be diminished during their Continuance in Office.

Section 2. The judicial Power shall extend to all Cases, in Law and Equity, arising under this Constitution, the Laws of the United States, and Treaties made, or which shall be made, under their Authority;—to all Cases affecting Ambassadors, other public Ministers and Consuls;—to all Cases of admiralty and maritime Jurisdiction;—to Controversies to which the United States shall be a Party;—to Controversies between two or more States;—between a State and Citizens of another State;—between Citizens of different States;—between Citizens of the same State claiming Lands under Grants of different States, and between a State, or the Citizens thereof, and foreign States, Citizens or Subjects.

In all Cases affecting Ambassadors, other public Ministers and Consuls, and those in which a State shall be Party, the supreme Court shall have original Jurisdiction. In all the other Cases before mentioned, the supreme Court shall have appellate Jurisdiction, both as to Law and Fact, with such Exceptions, and under such Regulations as the Congress shall make.

The Trial of all Crimes, except in Cases of Impeachment, shall be by Jury; and such Trial shall be held in the State where the said Crimes shall have been committed; but when not committed within any State, the Trial shall be at such Place or Places as the Congress may by Law have directed.

Section 3. Treason against the United States, shall consist only in levying War against them, or in adhering to their Enemies, giving them Aid and Comfort. No Person shall be convicted of Treason unless on the Testimony of two Witnesses to the same overt Act, or on Confession in open Court.

The Congress shall have Power to declare the Punishment of Treason, but no Attainder of Treason shall work Corruption of Blood, or Forfeiture except during the Life of the Person attainted.

Article IV

Section 1. Full Faith and Credit shall be given in each State to the public Acts, Records, and judicial Proceedings of every other State. And the Congress may by general Laws prescribe the Manner in which such Acts, Records, and Proceedings shall be proved, and the Effect thereof.

Section 2. The Citizens of each State shall be entitled to all Privileges and Immunities of Citizens in the several States.

A Person charged in any State with Treason, Felony, or other Crime, who shall flee from Justice, and be found in another State, shall on Demand of the executive Authority of the State from which he fled, be delivered up, to be removed to the State having Jurisdiction of the Crime.

No Person held to Service or Labour in one State, under the Laws thereof, escaping into another, shall, in Consequence of any Law or Regulation therein, be discharged from such Service or Labour, but shall be delivered up on Claim of the Party to whom such Service or Labour may be due.

Section 3. New States may be admitted by the Congress into this Union; but no new States shall be formed or erected within the Jurisdiction of any other State; nor any State be formed by the Junction of two or more States, or Parts of States, without the Consent of the Legislatures of the States concerned as well as of the Congress.

The Congress shall have Power to dispose of and make all needful Rules and Regulations respecting the Territory or other Property belonging to the United States; and nothing in this Constitution shall be so construed as to Prejudice any Claims of the United States, or of any particular State.

Section 4. The United States shall guarantee to every State in this Union a Republican Form of Government, and shall protect each of them against Invasion; and on Application of the Legislature, or of the Executive (when the Legislature cannot be convened) against domestic Violence.

Article V

The Congress, whenever two thirds of both Houses shall deem it necessary, shall propose Amendments to this Constitution, or, on the Application of the Legislatures of two thirds of the several States, shall call a Convention for proposing Amendments, which, in either Case, shall be valid to all Intents and Purposes, as Part of this Constitution, when ratified by the Legislatures of three fourths of the several States, or by Conventions in three fourths thereof, as the one or the other Mode of Ratification may be proposed by the Congress; Provided that no Amendment which may be made prior to the Year One thousand eight hundred and eight shall in any Manner affect the first and fourth Clauses in the Ninth Section of the first Article; and that no State, without its Consent, shall be deprived of its equal Suffrage in the Senate.

Article VI

All Debts contracted and Engagements entered into, before the Adoption of this Constitution, shall be as valid against the United States under this Constitution, as under the Confederation.

This Constitution, and the Laws of the United States which shall be made in Pursuance thereof; and all Treaties made, or which shall be made, under the Authority of the United States, shall be the supreme Law of the Land; and the Judges in every State shall be bound thereby, any Thing in the Constitution or Laws of any State to the Contrary not with-standing.

The Senators and Representatives before mentioned, and the Members of the several State Legislatures, and all executive and judicial Officers, both of the United States and of the several States, shall be bound by Oath or Affirmation, to support this Constitution; but no religious Test shall ever be required as a Qualification to any Office or public Trust under the United States.

Article VII

The Ratification of the Conventions of nine States, shall be sufficient for the Establishment of this Constitution between the States so ratifying the Same.

Done in Convention by the Unanimous Consent of the States present the Seventeenth Day of September in the Year of our Lord one thousand seven hundred and Eighty seven and of the Independence of the United States of America the Twelfth

In witness whereof We have hereunto subscribed our Names,

George Washington—President and deputy from Virginia

New Hampshire: John Langdon, Nicholas Gilman

Massachusetts: Nathaniel Gorham, Rufus King

Connecticut: William Samuel Johnson, Roger Sherman

New York: Alexander Hamilton

New Jersey: William Livingston, David Brearly, William Paterson, Jonathan Dayton

Pennsylvania: Benjamin Franklin, Thomas Mifflin, Robert Morris, George Clymer, Thomas FitzSimons, Jared Ingersoll, James Wilson, Gouverneur Morris

Delaware: George Read, Gunning Bedford, Jr., John Dickinson, Richard Bassett, Jacob Broom

Maryland: James McHenry, Daniel of Saint Thomas Jenifer, Daniel Carroll

Virginia: John Blair, James Madison, Jr.

North Carolina: William Blount, Richard Dobbs Spaight, Hugh Williamson

South Carolina: John Rutledge, Charles Cotesworth Pinckney, Charles Pinckney, Pierce Butler

Georgia: William Few, Abraham Baldwin

Source: *The Pennsylvania Packet*, **September 19, 1787**

AMENDMENTS TO THE U.S. CONSTITUTION

The first Ten Amendments to the United States Constitution are the
Bill of Rights.
The Bill of Rights was ratified as part of a gentlemen's agreement among our
Founding Fathers. There was resistance to the approval of the United States
Constitution by Thomas Jefferson and others because too much power was
given to the Federal government, and American citizens were unprotected. The
Constitution was ratified in 1788, and the Federalists kept their word and
ratified the Bill of Rights in 1791 to protect the individual
rights of American citizens.

The Bill of Rights

- First Amendment – Establishment Clause, Free Exercise Clause;
freedom of speech, of the press, Freedom of Religion, and of assembly;
right to petition.
Congress shall make no law respecting an establishment of religion, or
prohibiting the free exercise thereof; or abridging the freedom of speech, or of
the press; or the right of the people peaceably to assemble, and to petition the
Government for a redress of grievances.

- Second Amendment – Militia (United States), Sovereign state,
Right to keep and bear arms.
A well-regulated Militia, being necessary to the security of a free State, the right
of the people to keep and bear Arms, shall not be infringed. [5][6]

- Third Amendment – Protection from quartering of troops.
No Soldier shall, in time of peace be quartered in any house, without the
consent of the Owner, nor in time of war, but in a manner to
be prescribed by law.

- Fourth Amendment – Protection from unreasonable search and seizure.
The right of the people to be secure in their persons, houses, papers, and
effects, against unreasonable searches and seizures, shall not be violated,
and no Warrants shall issue, but upon probable cause, supported by Oath
or affirmation, and particularly describing the place to be searched, and the
persons or things to be seized.

- <u>Fifth Amendment</u> – <u>due process</u>, <u>double jeopardy</u>, <u>self-incrimination</u>, <u>eminent domain</u>.

No person shall be held to answer for any capital, or otherwise infamous crime, unless on a presentment or indictment of a Grand Jury, except in cases arising in the land or naval forces, or in the Militia, when in actual service in time of War or public danger; nor shall any person be subject for the same offence to be twice put in jeopardy of life or limb; nor shall be compelled in any criminal case to be a witness against himself, nor be deprived of life, liberty, or property, without due process of law; nor shall private property be taken for public use, without just compensation.

- <u>Sixth Amendment</u> – <u>Trial by jury</u> and <u>rights of the accused</u>; <u>Confrontation Clause</u>, <u>speedy trial</u>, <u>public trial</u>, <u>right to counsel</u>.

In all criminal prosecutions, the accused shall enjoy the right to a speedy and public trial, by an impartial jury of the State and district where in the crime shall have been committed, which district shall have been previously ascertained by law, and to be informed of the nature and cause of the accusation; to be confronted with the witnesses against him; to have compulsory process for obtaining witnesses in his favor, and to have the Assistance of Counsel for his defense.

- <u>Seventh Amendment</u> – <u>Civil</u> trial by jury.

In suits at common law, where the value in controversy shall exceed twenty dollars, the right of trial by jury shall be preserved, and no fact tried by a jury, shall be otherwise re-examined in any court of the United States, than according to the rules of the common law.

- <u>Eighth Amendment</u> – Prohibition of <u>excessive bail</u> and <u>cruel and unusual punishment</u>.

Excessive bail shall not be required, nor excessive fines imposed, nor cruel and unusual punishments inflicted.

- <u>Ninth Amendment</u> – Protection of rights not specifically enumerated in the Bill of Rights.

The enumeration in the Constitution, of certain rights, shall not be construed to deny or disparage others retained by the people.

- <u>Tenth Amendment</u> – Powers of States and people.

The powers not delegated to the United States by the Constitution, nor prohibited by it to the States, are reserved to the States respectively, or to the people.

AMENDMENTS 11–27 TO THE CONSTITUTION
OF THE UNITED STATES

*This list includes **Amendments 11 to 27**, and provides a brief historical background on the reason for its inclusion as an Amendment to the United States Constitution.*

THE ELEVENTH AMENDMENT
This amendment arose from states' rights, and was designed to keep suits between states and their citizens out of federal courts.
Ratification was completed on February 7, 1795.

The Judicial power of the United States shall not be construed to extend to any suit in law or equity, commenced or prosecuted against one of the United States by Citizens of another State, or by Citizens or Subjects of any Foreign State.

THE TWELFTH AMENDMENT
The Twelfth Amendment requires separate balloting in the Electoral College for President and Vice President, to avoid the difficulties encountered when the 1804 election was thrown into the House of Representatives. It took 36 ballots before Thomas Jefferson was chosen as the third president of the United States! Ratification was completed on June 15, 1804.

The Electors shall meet in their respective states, and vote by ballot for President and Vice President, one of whom, at least, shall not be an inhabitant of the same state with themselves; they shall name in their ballots the person voted for as President, and in distinct ballots the person voted for as Vice President, and they shall make distinct lists of all persons voted for as President, and of all persons voted for as Vice President, and of the number of votes for each, which lists they shall sign and certify, and transmit sealed to the seat of the government of the United States, directed to the President of the Senate;—The President of the Senate shall, in the presence of the Senate and House of Representatives, open all the certificates and the votes shall then be counted;—The person having the greatest number of votes for President, shall be the President, if such number be a majority of the whole number of Electors appointed; and if no person have such majority, then from the persons having the highest numbers not exceeding three on the list of those voted for as President, the House of Representatives shall choose immediately, by ballot, the President. But in choosing the President, the votes shall be taken by states, the representation from each state having one vote; a quorum for this purpose shall consist of a member or members from two-thirds of the states, and a majority of all the states shall be necessary to a choice. And if the House of Representatives shall not choose a President whenever the right of choice shall devolve upon them, before the fourth day of March next following, then the Vice President shall act as President, as in the case of the death or other constitutional disability of the President. The person having the greatest number of votes as Vice President, shall be the Vice President, if such number be a majority of the whole number of Electors appointed, and if no person have a majority, then from the two highest numbers on the list, the Senate shall choose the Vice President; a quorum for the purpose shall consist of two-thirds of the whole number of Senators, and a majority of the whole number shall be necessary to a choice. But no person constitutionally ineligible to the office of President shall be eligible to that of Vice President of the United States.

THE THIRTEENTH AMENDMENT
The Thirteenth Amendment followed the Civil War and put an end to African-American slavery.
Ratification was completed on December 6, 1865.

Section 1. Neither slavery nor involuntary servitude, except as a punishment for crime whereof the party shall have been duly convicted, shall exist within the United States, or any place subject to their jurisdiction.
Section 2. Congress shall have power to enforce this article by appropriate legislation.

THE FOURTEENTH AMENDMENT
The Fourteenth Amendment was the second of three amendments following the Civil War. This amendment defined American citizenship, but also placed restrictions on former Confederates. This amendment is often quoted by the Supreme Court as providing "equal protection" to all citizens and was referenced in the 2000 Florida recount decision.
Ratification was completed on July 9, 1868.

Section 1. All persons born or naturalized in the United States, and subject to the jurisdiction thereof, are citizens of the United States and of the State wherein they reside. No State shall make or enforce any law which shall abridge the privileges or immunities of citizens of the United States; nor shall any State deprive any person of life, liberty, or property, without due process of law; nor deny to any person within its jurisdiction the equal protection of the laws.

Section 2. Representatives shall be apportioned among the several States according to their respective numbers, counting the whole number of persons in each State, excluding Indians not taxed. But when the right to vote at any election for the choice of electors for President and Vice President of the United States, Representatives in Congress, the Executive and Judicial officers of a State, or the members of the Legislature thereof, is denied to any of the male inhabitants of such State, being twenty-one years of age and citizens of the United States, or in any way abridged, except for participation in rebellion, or other crime, the basis of representation therein shall be reduced in the proportion which the number of such male citizens shall bear to the whole number of male citizens twenty-one years of age in such State.

Section 3. No person shall be a Senator or Representative in Congress, or elector of President and Vice President, or hold any office, civil or military, under the United States, or under any State, who, having previously taken an oath, as a member of Congress, or as an officer of the United States, or as a member of any State legislature, or as an executive or judicial officer of any State, to support the Constitution of the United States, shall have engaged in insurrection or rebellion against the same, or given aid or comfort to the enemies thereof. But Congress may by a vote of two-thirds of each House, remove such disability.

Section 4. The validity of the public debt of the United States, authorized by law, including debts incurred for payment of pensions and bounties for services in suppressing insurrection or rebellion, shall not be questioned. But neither the United States nor any State shall assume or pay any debt or obligation incurred in aid of insurrection or rebellion against the United States, or any claim for the loss or emancipation of any slave; but all such debts, obligations and claims shall be held illegal and void.

Section 5. The Congress shall have power to enforce, by appropriate legislation, the provisions of this article.

THE FIFTEENTH AMENDMENT

The Fifteenth Amendment was the third amendment following the Civil War that addressed the issue of African-American slavery. This amendment prohibited states from denying the right to vote because of a person's race or because a person had been a slave. Even with the ratification of this amendment, Indians and women were still not yet allowed to vote! The amendment was ratified in February of 1870.

Section 1. The right of citizens of the United States to vote shall not be denied or abridged by the United States or by any State on account of race, color, or previous condition of servitude.
Section 2. The Congress shall have power to enforce this article by appropriate legislation.

THE SIXTEENTH AMENDMENT
The Sixteenth Amendment began the federal income tax!
Ratification was completed on February 3, 1913.

The Congress shall have power to lay and collect taxes on incomes, from whatever source derived, without apportionment among the several States, and without regard to any census or enumeration.

THE SEVENTEENTH AMENDMENT
The Seventeenth Amendment allowed election of Senators directly
by popular vote.
Ratification was completed on April 8, 1913.

The Senate of the United States shall be composed of two Senators from each State, elected by the people thereof, for six years; and each Senator shall have one vote. The electors in each State shall have the qualifications requisite for electors of the most numerous branch of the State legislatures. When vacancies happen in the representation of any State in the Senate, the executive authority of such State shall issue writs of election to fill such vacancies: Provided, That the legislature of any State may empower the executive thereof to make temporary appointments until the people fill the vacancies by election as the legislature may direct.
This amendment shall not be so construed as to affect the election or term of any Senator chosen before it becomes valid as part of the Constitution.

THE EIGHTEENTH AMENDMENT
The Eighteenth Amendment began the Prohibition of alcohol.
This amendment was ratified in January 1919.

Section 1. After one year from the ratification of this article the manufacture, sale, or transportation of intoxicating liquors within, the importation thereof into, or the exportation thereof from the United States and all territory subject to the jurisdiction thereof for beverage purposes is hereby prohibited.

Section 2. The Congress and the several States shall have concurrent power to enforce this article by appropriate legislation.

Section 3. This article shall be inoperative unless it shall have been ratified as an amendment to the Constitution by the legislatures of the several States, as provided in the Constitution, within seven years from the date of the submission hereof to the States by the Congress.

THE NINETEENTH AMENDMENT
The Nineteenth Amendment granted women suffrage or the right to vote. This amendment was ratified by August of 1920.

The right of citizens of the United States to vote shall not be denied or abridged by the United States or by any State on account of sex. Congress shall have power to enforce this article by appropriate legislation.

THE TWENTIETH AMENDMENT
The Twentieth Amendment, commonly called the "Lame Duck Amendment," shortened the period between Election Day and Inauguration Day from March 4 to January 20 for the president, and to January 3 for the opening session for Congress. This was ratified February 6, 1933.

Section 1. The terms of the President and Vice President shall end at noon on the 20th day of January, and the terms of Senators and Representatives at noon on the 3d day of January, of the years in which such terms would have ended if this article had not been ratified; and the terms of their successors shall then begin.

Section 2. The Congress shall assemble at least once in every year, and such meeting shall begin at noon on the 3d day of January, unless they shall by law appoint a different day.

Section 3. If, at the time fixed for the beginning of the term of the President, the President-elect shall have died, the Vice President-elect shall become President. If a President shall not have been chosen before the time fixed for the beginning of his term, or if the President-elect shall have failed to qualify, then the Vice President-elect shall act as President until a President shall have qualified; and the Congress may by law provide for the case wherein neither a President-elect nor a Vice President-elect shall have qualified, declaring who shall then act as President, or the manner in which one who is to act shall be selected, and such person shall act accordingly until a President or Vice President shall have qualified.

Section 4. The Congress may by law provide for the case of the death of any of the persons from whom the House of Representatives may choose a President whenever the right of choice shall have devolved upon them, and for the case of the death of any of the persons from whom the Senate may choose a Vice President whenever the right of choice shall have devolved upon them.

Section 5. Sections 1 and 2 shall take effect on the 15th day of October following the ratification of this article.

Section 6. This article shall be inoperative unless it shall have been ratified as an amendment to the Constitution by the legislatures of three-fourths of the several States within seven years from the date of its submission.

THE TWENTY-FIRST AMENDMENT
This amendment repealed Prohibition and was ratified on December 5, 1933.

Section 1. The eighteenth article of amendment to the Constitution of the United States is hereby repealed.

Section 2. The transportation or importation into any State, Territory, or possession of the United States for delivery or use therein of intoxicating liquors, in violation of the laws thereof, is hereby prohibited.

Section 3. This article shall be inoperative unless it shall have been ratified as an amendment to the Constitution by conventions in the several States, as provided in the Constitution, within seven years from the date of the submission hereof to the States by the Congress.

THE TWENTY-SECOND AMENDMENT
This amendment began the two-term limit of the U.S. president and was ratified February 27, 1951.

Section 1. No person shall be elected to the office of the President more than twice, and no person who has held the office of President, or acted as President, for more than two years of a term to which some other person was elected President shall be elected to the office of the President more than once. But this article shall not apply to any person holding the office of President when this article was proposed by the Congress, and shall not prevent any person who may be holding the office of President, or acting as President, during the term within which this article becomes operative from holding the office of President or acting as President during the remainder of such term.

Section 2. This article shall be inoperative unless it shall have been ratified as an amendment to the Constitution by the legislatures of three-fourths of the several states within seven years from the date of its submission to the states by the Congress.

THE TWENTY-THIRD AMENDMENT
This amendment gave the presidential vote to Washington, D.C., and was ratified March 29, 1961.

Section 1. The District constituting the seat of government of the United States shall appoint in such manner as the Congress may direct: A number of electors of President and Vice President equal to the whole number of Senators and Representatives in Congress to which the District would be entitled if it were a state, but in no event more than the least populous state; they shall be in addition to those appointed by the states, but they shall be considered, for the purposes of the election of President and Vice President, to be electors appointed by a state; and they shall meet in the District and perform such duties as provided by the twelfth article of amendment.
Section 2. The Congress shall have power to enforce this article by appropriate legislation.

THE TWENTY-FOURTH AMENDMENT
This amendment nullified the poll tax and was ratified January 23, 1964.

Section 1. The right of citizens of the United States to vote in any primary or other election for President or Vice President, for electors for President or Vice President, or for Senator or Representative in Congress, shall not be denied or abridged by the United States or any state by reason of failure to pay any poll tax or other tax.
Section 2. The Congress shall have power to enforce this article by appropriate legislation.

THE TWENTY-FIFTH AMENDMENT
This amendment has to do with presidential succession and was ratified February 10, 1967.

Section 1. In case of the removal of the President from office or of his death or resignation, the Vice President shall become President.
Section 2. Whenever there is a vacancy in the office of the Vice President, the President shall nominate a Vice President who shall take office upon confirmation by a majority vote of both Houses of Congress.

Section 3. Whenever the President transmits to the President pro tempore of the Senate and the Speaker of the House of Representatives his written declaration that he is unable to discharge the powers and duties of his office, and until he transmits to them a written declaration to the contrary, such powers and duties shall be discharged by the Vice President as Acting President.

Section 4. Whenever the Vice President and a majority of either the principal officers of the executive departments or of such other body as Congress may by law provide, transmit to the President pro tempore of the Senate and the Speaker of the House of Representatives their written declaration that the President is unable to discharge the powers and duties of his office, the Vice President shall immediately assume the powers and duties of the office as Acting President.

Thereafter, when the President transmits to the President pro tempore of the Senate and the Speaker of the House of Representatives his written declaration that no inability exists, he shall resume the powers and duties of his office unless the Vice President and a majority of either the principal officers of the executive department or of such other body as Congress may by law provide, transmit within four days to the President pro tempore of the Senate and the Speaker of the House of Representatives their written declaration that the President is unable to discharge the powers and duties of his office. Thereupon Congress shall decide the issue, assembling within forty-eight hours for that purpose if not in session. If the Congress, within twenty-one days after receipt of the latter written declaration, or, if Congress is not in session, within twenty-one days after Congress is required to assemble, determines by two-thirds vote of both Houses that the President is unable to discharge the powers and duties of his office, the Vice President shall continue to discharge the same as Acting President; otherwise, the President shall resume the powers and duties of his office.

THE TWENTY-SIXTH AMENDMENT
This amendment gave the right to vote to eighteen-year-old citizens and was ratified July 1, 1971.

Section 1. The right of citizens of the United States, who are 18 years of age or older, to vote, shall not be denied or abridged by the United States or any state on account of age.

Section 2. The Congress shall have the power to enforce this article by appropriate legislation.

THE TWENTY-SEVENTH AMENDMENT
This amendment concerned compensation of Members of Congress and was ratified May 7, 1992.

No law varying the compensation for the services of the Senators and Representatives shall take effect until an election of Representatives shall have intervened.

CHAPTER SIX

DEFENSE—THE SINGLE MOST IMPORTANT FUNCTION OF THE U.S. GOVERNMENT

> *"A veteran—whether active duty, retired, or national guard or reserve—is someone who, at one point in his or her life, wrote a blank check made payable to 'The United States of America,' for an amount of 'up to and including my life.' That is honor, and there are way too many people in this country who no longer understand it."*
>
> **—Author Unknown**

THE GREATEST GENERATION

Of the sixteen million soldiers who served in World War II, there are just ten percent of them still living today. These folks are dying at the rate of more than 850 per day. The average age of those who are still living is ninety-two. "The Greatest Generation" of Americans seldom spoke of their war years once they returned home in 1945 and 1946. Perhaps these soldiers wanted to forget their experience and get on with their lives, just grateful that they had survived and not wanting to dwell on the friends they had left behind. Or perhaps they just saw their service to their country in the same light that our founding fathers had, which was that it was simply their duty to serve. It may be different for each of them, but what is certainly common among *all* of them is that once they returned home in 1945 and 1946, they were ready to simply get on with their lives and not dwell on the past. I have had the good fortune to know many of these soldiers from "the Greatest Generation," and to a person they each have exemplified the exact same humility and quiet sense of duty to their nation and to their families.

While I was writing this book, I had a long conversation with Russell E. (Eugene) Gilmer, one of the individuals to whom this book is dedicated. Gene (his middle name is Eugene, and he prefers to go by Gene) is my stepfather. My own father died when I was four years old, and my mother remarried when I was eleven. Gene saw me through those teenage years, which as everyone knows are not always easy. During my recent conversation with Gene, he shared many of his experiences from World War II. Gene had never shared these stories while we were growing up. We began the conversation with a discussion about this book, for I had sent excerpts from the book to all of my clients in late June 2009. Gene is very supportive of this work and appreciates that someone is boldly advancing the causes of Liberty and Freedom. Gene explained that it is difficult for him to understand much of what has transpired in our government these past few years, for as he says, "*It makes no sense.*" Gene often simply turns off the television.

Gene and four of his friends drove to Indianapolis and enlisted into the military shortly after graduating from high school in 1941. This was the course of action most young men took during this time in our history. Gene saw World War II in both the European and Pacific fronts. Gene ended up in the Navy and was one of the crew on a landing craft that shuttled the soldiers back and forth between England and the beaches of Omaha and Utah at Normandy during the D-Day invasion. Gene experienced all-out war right before his eyes for several days as his ship shuttled soldiers from England to France. Once Europe was liberated and Germany defeated, Gene's group was sent to the Pacific via the United States to make ready for an invasion of Japan.

> *"As it turned out, the atomic bomb ended the war sooner than most thought would be the case; however, that event didn't take Gene out of harm's way."*

Before arriving safely in a U.S. port, Gene's ship was caught in a fierce hurricane off the Carolina coast, where they were forced to "ride it out" for several days before coming ashore. Ironically, Gene said the experience with the hurricane could actually compete with some of the worst battles of the war. After a short stay in the United States, Gene's group headed for Japan through the Panama Canal. As it turned out, the atomic bomb ended the war sooner than most thought would be the case; however, that event didn't take Gene out of harm's way. He was among those sent in to clear Tokyo Harbor of mines to make way for the arrival of Douglas MacArthur on the *USS Missouri* for the signing of the peace treaty with Japan. Gene explained that they first sent in two wooden-hull ships (wooden hulls were used because steel hulls would attract the mines) with a cable stretched between them below the surface to cut loose the mines, allowing them to surface to the top of the water. Once the mines were floating free, the sailors shot them with high-powered 30-30 rifles to detonate the mines. With this task finished, Gene's group sailed home for America via Hawaii. Gene still has a painting of his ship that one of his fellow sailors had painted while they were in port at Honolulu after the war. "Diamond Head" appears in the background of the scene. Gene paid his shipmate $10 for the work.

...as George described it: "I mashed down on top of the driver's foot with all my might, and stayed there until we were ashore."

This book is also dedicated to George Huffman, my business partner of several years in the insurance business. George had already graduated from Purdue University before World War II began. George was in the U.S. Army Artillery and was responsible for an eight-inch howitzer gun. These guns could shoot several miles. George was among those who landed at Normandy and liberated Europe. George once told me a story about the day they went ashore at Normandy. Once the ramp on the ship was dropped, you were ordered to hit the gas at full throttle and remain at full throttle until you were on dry land. Otherwise, the engine might stall or die, leaving you "dead in the water." The soldier who was driving the vehicle in which George was a passenger took his foot off the accelerator when the cold water from the Atlantic Ocean "hit him." This could have meant a certain end to the landing for their group. So when the driver pulled his foot back from the gas pedal, George simply took his left foot and, as George described it, "I mashed down on top of the driver's foot with all my might, and stayed there until we were ashore."

"The Battle of the Bulge became the single biggest and bloodiest battle that American forces experienced in World War II."

George's division marched through France, liberated Europe, and then went on to fight in "Hitler's last stand," which was the Battle of the Bulge in Belgium. No one expected Hitler to make this attack, and the entire Allied

Army was caught by surprise when it occurred. George explained to me one day that with all military operations, there is a certain order that is strictly adhered to. As an army advances, the artillery is always shooting in their forward position as they progress. George said that in mid-December 1944, his group got an order from on high to turn their guns 180 degrees and commence firing. George's commanding officer couldn't believe the order, for normally that would mean firing on your own forces as they were coming up behind you. When the order was questioned, the reply very quickly came back that they were to do precisely as ordered. As it turned out, German forces were surrounding the Allies by making a sudden advance on the Allied lines. This created a bulge (thus the name of the battle) in the Allied line, allowing the Germans to be at their rear. The Battle of the Bulge became the single biggest and bloodiest battle that American forces experienced in World War II, according to Wikipedia.org.

The other two individuals to whom this book is dedicated are J. Ben Good and Gordon Laymon. J. Ben Good served in the Navy in World War II. Ben served on a patrol craft (or PC boat) in the South Pacific. These patrol crafts were used in hunting down Japanese submarines and dropping depth charges. Ben's wife Elizabeth waited patiently at home with their infant son Ted for Ben's return after the war. The Laymon family has been involved in our local telephone company for over three generations. During World War II, there was a desperate need in the military for every skill imaginable. One such area requiring specialized skill was the communication field through the Signal Corps. The need for expertise in this area led Gordon's dad, Robert Laymon, to volunteer despite the fact that he left a wife and three sons at home. Robert served in the South Pacific and was among those who often went in ahead of the main invasion force, using stealth tactics to string cable wire to provide communication on or between islands. Gordon Laymon, Robert's son, served our nation during the Korean War. He followed in the footsteps of his father, serving in the Signal Corps for two years during that war.

Our eldest son Aaron graduated from high school in May 2000. Shortly after graduation, Aaron came home and announced that he had joined the army. Some of the family were upset that Aaron had joined the service. I was concerned but not in any way upset. I congratulated Aaron on joining the army and explained to him that I felt that there was a void in my life by not having served our nation in the military. Aaron served three years active duty and spent one of those years in Korea, just south of the 38th parallel near the DMZ (demilitarized zone). After Aaron's three years of active duty service, he reenlisted in the Indiana National Guard. Just about the time his National Guard service was to expire, Aaron's group was called up for a tour to Iraq, where he spent a year in the Ramadi region outside Baghdad.

Upon Aaron's return from Iraq, he reenlisted for another term in the Indiana National Guard.

> *"'We the People' owe these men, and other Americans just like them, a huge debt of gratitude."*

Each of the men above was willing to do whatever was asked of them to defend Liberty and Freedom—not just for America, but quite literally for all mankind around the world. ***"We the People"*** owe these men, and other Americans just like them, a huge debt of gratitude.

FROM THE U.S. CONSTITUTION

> ***"We the People"*** *of the United States, in Order to form a more perfect Union, establish Justice, insure domestic Tranquility, provide for the common defence, promote the general Welfare, and secure the Blessings of Liberty to ourselves and our Posterity, do ordain and establish this Constitution for the United States of America.*

> *"The United States will always come to the aid of her friends and will most certainly always protect her interests, both foreign and domestic."*

One of the few legitimate purposes, and certainly *the* single most important purpose for, and responsibility of, the U.S. federal government is to *"provide for the common defense"* of the nation of the United States. The military comprises between 25 percent and 50 percent of total spending by the federal government, depending upon how you choose to allocate interest on the federal debt, veterans' benefits, military pensions, and so on. *Direct* military costs are 20 to 25 percent of the total annual U.S. federal budget. In the reorganization of the government, there will be the same thorough top-to-bottom review of effectiveness and efficiencies related to military spending that should always accompany any reorganization. Changes should include a revisit of where the U.S. military is stationed overseas and why they are stationed in each of these foreign lands. The United States will always come to the aid of her friends and will most certainly always protect her interests, both foreign and domestic. However, from this day forward, she can no longer afford, nor should others any longer look for her, to serve as the "military police" for the world. The U.S. government continues to have 53,000 military personnel in Germany and 39,000 in Japan. World War II ended sixty-four years ago. It is time to bring most all of these troops home.

"We the People" of the United States are now in the process of learning to face our inherent limitations and to live within our "collective means" as a nation. The United States can no longer afford to protect the world militarily. The U.S. military establishment cannot and will not be exempt from the financial austerity that our entire nation must now endure. However, cuts in the Defense Department will not come from the troops or military readiness, but rather from the endless waste that our present group of corrupt, career, elitist politicians have inappropriately buried in the defense budget. A great example would be the recent purchase of the Gulfstream jets for members of Congress to fly around in. Fortunately, there was such an outcry from the American public that this expenditure was ultimately stricken from the bill and rescinded by the U.S. Congress.

> *"By calling attention to 'a well-regulated militia,' the 'security' of the nation, and the right of each citizen 'to keep and bear arms,' our founding fathers recognized the essentially civilian nature of our economy. Although it is extremely unlikely that the fears of governmental tyranny, which gave rise to the Second Amendment, will ever be a major danger to our nation, the Amendment still remains an important declaration of our basic civilian-military relationships, in which every citizen must be ready to participate in the defense of his country. For that reason, I believe the Second Amendment will always be important."*
>
> **—Senator John F. Kennedy**, 1960

This quote by Senator, and soon to be President, John F. Kennedy is in support of the Second Amendment to the U.S. Constitution. Isn't it interesting that fifty years ago, J.F.K.'s quote includes a statement that "*it is extremely unlikely that the fears of governmental tyranny, which gave rise to the Second Amendment, will ever be a major danger to our nation,*" yet in our America of today in the year 2012, gun and ammunition manufacturers can't keep pace with the demand for either of these items? In his 1960 quote,

Senator Kennedy makes it clear that the right to bear arms under the Second Amendment was given so that the people could protect themselves "from fears of governmental tyranny." This is an important admission by a senator, and soon to be president, of the United States. Thomas Jefferson, one of the original revolutionaries, had a clear understanding of the true purpose for the Second Amendment and had this to say about it:

"The strongest reason for people to retain the right to keep and bear arms is, as a last resort, to protect themselves against tyranny in government."

—Thomas Jefferson

"The recent skyrocketing sale of both guns and ammunition should give anyone serving in government pause as they go about the 'people's' business."

In our 225-year history as a nation, ***"We the People"*** have never taken up arms against our government (with the exception of the Civil War, an event that many founders feared might take place). This fact is an awesome testament to our form of government and to the founders who created our great Republic. Nevertheless, it doesn't hurt for our current elected leaders to be reminded, and to fully understand, that the people have the right under our Constitution to protect themselves against a tyrannical government. The recent skyrocketing sale of both guns and ammunition should give anyone serving in government pause as they go about the *"people's"* business. The weapons and ammunition were not bought these past few years by the American people for protection against any sort of "foreign enemy." Americans continue to be an independent people who, by and large, deeply value their Liberty, their rights, and their freedoms, which are given them by God and are secured under our Constitution. Any person, or any governmental body of people, who attempt to threaten or even to ponder threatening those Liberties, rights, and freedoms "of the people" would do well to remember and to continually bear in mind this unconditional right of *"We the People"* in America.

> *"we could have avoided the attacks of 9/11 by having knocked out Osama bin Laden when we had the chance, for bin Laden was at war with us well in advance of 9/11/2001."*

As we transition back to a truly free society from our current status as a socialist state, and begin living within our means, we will out of necessity be required to carefully consider how our military dollars are spent. First and foremost, the federal government's responsibility is to protect the American people. In this regard, we can and must improve our intelligence gathering, especially in light of the enemies that we now face. On this matter, we can learn a great deal from our Israeli friends. Since its creation more than sixty years ago, Israel has found it essential to be incredibly resourceful—simply to survive. They are a tiny nation and are completely surrounded by much larger nations who would like nothing more than to see them disappear. Consequently, Israel has developed a very sophisticated intelligence apparatus. Israel is a friend of the United States. We need to study and learn all that we can from them. We must pull in our horns and be less interventionist. This is not to say that we should be isolationist; however, in the future, we must be more careful in picking our battles and "entangling" ourselves in the affairs of other nations. Thomas Jefferson on March 4, 1801, urged that the United States must have *"peace, commerce, and honest friendship with all nations—entangling alliances with none."* His words are as true today as they were then. Who knows, perhaps if we had been more successful at national intelligence prior to 2001, we could have avoided the attacks of 9/11 by having knocked out Osama bin Laden when we had the chance, for bin Laden was at war with us well in advance of 9/11/2001.

SOLUTIONS FOR A MORE PEACEFUL WORLD
AND A MORE SECURE AMERICA

1. Immediately bring as many of our military personnel home from the soil of foreign nations as is possible within the confines of maintaining the security of the United States.
2. Close as many military bases in foreign nations as is possible within the same confines as above.
3. Redeploy the troops from above within the United States in order to secure our borders and to protect the sovereignty of the United States.
4. Immediately put all foreign nations on notice that the United States will no longer be serving as the "policeman of the world."
5. Immediately cease and desist from providing aid to foreign nations, explaining that we are broke.
6. Begin immediately beefing up our national intelligence community to better protect the United States from all enemies, both foreign and domestic.

CHAPTER SEVEN

FREEDOM, LIBERTY, AND RONALD REAGAN

TIMING IS EVERYTHING

"Reagan earnestly desired that our nation would one day turn back to and embrace the fundamental principles of our founders. Ronald Reagan was a true American patriot."

President Ronald Reagan understood what a tremendous gift our founders had given us. Reagan was a serious student of the Constitution of the United States, and he had studied and therefore understood our founding fathers. He knew how they thought, and he understood what their intentions were for this, our great democratic experiment. Reagan earnestly desired that our nation would one day turn back to and embrace the fundamental principles of our founders. Ronald Reagan was a true American patriot. While Reagan was on the right track, it turned out that he was just a little ahead of his time. In 1980, the country had not yet wandered far enough away from our founders' principles, nor had its people suffered enough pain and discomfort, to arouse the masses into taking action. That has all now changed—what a difference thirty years can make.

"If we are not willing and able to get control of our own reckless behavior, and do so very soon, the result this time around will be that we will lose our very Liberty and

Freedom and along with it, the last chance we will ever have to redeem our great nation."

Just as Ronald Reagan has been proven correct in most all of his positions, despite being ahead of his time by some thirty years, it could very well turn out that the dire warnings in this book along with the proposed solutions will likewise be proven correct, yet ahead of their time. I hope this will not be the case, for the stakes are much higher this time around. The United States during its entire history and up to Ronald Reagan's time had always been essentially a creditor nation, allowing us the luxury of time to mend our ways. This time is different. If we are not willing and able to get control of our own reckless behavior, and do so very soon, the result this time around will be that we will lose our very Liberty and Freedom and along with it, the last chance we will ever have to redeem our great nation. ***"We the People"*** are now forced to make some extraordinarily tough choices. Here, Reagan gives us a chilling reminder of our duties as Americans:

Ronald Reagan
1911 to 2004

"Freedom is never more than one generation away from extinction. We didn't pass it to our children in the bloodstream. It must be fought for, protected, and handed on to them to do the same, or one day we will spend our sunset years telling our

*children and our children's children what it was once like in
the United States where men were free."*

—**Ronald Reagan**, 1911–2004,
fortieth president of the United States (1981–1989)

What Choice Will You Make?

We now find ourselves at a critical juncture, an important moment of decision in our nation's history. We can ignore our reckless and insane fiscal mistakes of the past and continue marching down the road to socialism *or* we can stop, seriously reflect upon what we are about to give up, and change our course back to one of Liberty, Freedom, and the commonsense principles that allowed *"We the People"* to create the most incredible miracle of all mankind. Making the latter choice will mean that we are choosing to honor the sacrifices of our founders and forefathers. It will also mean that we choose to rescue the future existence of our great nation from the jaws of an otherwise certain death. It is, in my view, the correct choice and the choice that I fervently hope and pray we will make as a nation. I know for a certainty it is the choice Ronald Reagan and our founders would make. It is also the choice that will require great courage and a commitment by *each of us* to once again become involved and to take an active role to help chart a course for our nation's future.

*"This is the last chance for each of us to redeem our great
nation."*

Continuing the march down the road to socialism is the easy choice and the lazy way out. It is also the choice that we have actually already made "by default" up to now, through our *apathy* and *complacency*. So doing nothing has actually been a choice by us—a very real and clear choice. Whether conscious or not, that choice has been one of willingly relinquishing our nation to the hands of people who desire to convert it to a socialist state. So this is your wake-up call. This is the last chance for each of us to redeem our great nation. What choice will *you* make? As you consider your choice, please bear in mind that Liberty, once lost, can never be regained.

John Adams lived from 1735 to 1826. He was the second president of the United States and the longest living ex-president until Ronald Reagan died at the age of 93 in 2004.

"A Constitution of Government once changed from Freedom, can never be restored. Liberty, once lost, is lost forever."

—**John Adams** to Abigail Adams, 1775

John Adams and Thomas Jefferson ended life as devoted correspondents.

They had been fierce political opponents during the early years of our Republic. Jefferson believed staunchly in protecting States' rights, while Adams was a devoted Federalist. Fortunately, the two reconciled in 1812. As Adams put it: "You and I ought not to die before we have explained ourselves to each other." They spent the rest of their lives writing fascinating letters back and forth. Remarkably, both men died within four hours of each other on the exact same day, July 4, 1826, that being the fiftieth anniversary to the day of their both having signed the Declaration of Independence.

Ronald Reagan and Lady Margaret Thatcher of Great Britain were great friends and political soul mates. They both governed during the same decade of the 1980s. Lady Thatcher, like Reagan, had a keen sense of humor. Perhaps this quote by Margaret Thatcher would help explain their affinity one for the other:

"The problem with socialism is that you eventually run out of other people's money."

—**Margaret Thatcher,** British Prime Minister, 1979–1990

"There are a thousand hacking at the branches of evil to one who is striking at the roots."

—**Henry David Thoreau** (1817–1862)

Why a separate chapter on President Ronald Reagan? Simply because many folks reading this book will have a personal memory of Ronald Reagan and can therefore relate to what he said and did. Reagan governed during "our time." This experience allows the reader to easily validate the ideals and principles held by our founders, because Reagan's governance was consistent with these original ideals and principles of our founders. The ideals and principles that our founders used in creating our great nation are *unchanging* and *timeless*. Reagan had "internalized" their lessons. I consider Ronald Reagan to be America's *last true patriot statesman*.

Below are several other favorite quotes from our late and beloved Ronald Reagan:

"Here's my strategy on the Cold War: We win, they lose."

"The most terrifying words in the English language are: I'm from the government, and I'm here to help."

"The trouble with our liberal friends is not that they're ignorant; it's just that they know so much that isn't so."

"Of the four wars in my lifetime, none came about because the U.S. was too strong."

"I have wondered at times about what the Ten Commandments would have looked like if Moses had run them through the U.S. Congress."

"The taxpayer: That's someone who works for the federal government but doesn't have to take the civil service examination."

"Government is like a baby: An alimentary canal with a big appetite at one end and no sense of responsibility at the other."

"The nearest thing to eternal life we will ever see on this earth is a government program."

"It has been said that politics is the second oldest profession. I have learned that it bears a striking resemblance to the first."

"Government's view of the economy could be summed up in a few short phrases: If it moves, tax it. If it keeps moving, regulate it. And if it stops moving, subsidize it."

"Politics is not a bad profession. If you succeed, there are many rewards; if you disgrace yourself, you can always write a book."

"No arsenal, or no weapon in the arsenals of the world, is as formidable as the will and moral courage of free men and women."

"If we ever forget that we're one nation under God, then we will be a nation gone under."

"If we lose Freedom here, there is no place to escape to. This is the last stand on Earth."

Reagan also liked to say:

"It is amazing how much you can accomplish if you don't care who gets the credit."

OTHER THOUGHTS BY OUR FOUNDERS, FOREFATHERS, AND GREAT THINKERS THAT ARE WORTH REMEMBERING:

"The issue today is the same as it has been throughout all history, whether man shall be allowed to govern himself or be ruled by a small elite."
—Thomas Jefferson

"The greatest tyrannies are always perpetrated in the name of the noblest causes."
—Thomas Paine

*"God grants Liberty only to those who love it, and
are always ready to guard and defend it."*
—Daniel Webster, 1834

*"The tyranny of a principal in an oligarchy is not so dangerous to
the public welfare as the apathy of a citizen in a democracy."*
—Montesquieu, 1748

"Tyranny is always better organized than Freedom."
—Charles Peguy.

"The ignorance of one voter in a democracy impairs the security of all."
—John F. Kennedy, 1963

*"In the end, more than they wanted Freedom, they wanted security.
They wanted a comfortable life, and they lost it all—security,
comfort, and Freedom. When ... the Freedom they wished for was
Freedom from responsibility, then Athens ceased to be free."*
—Sir Edward Gibbon (1737–1794)

*"The two enemies of the people are criminals and government, so
let us tie the second down with the chains of the Constitution so
the second will not become the legalized version of the first."*
—Thomas Jefferson

*"I believe there are more instances of the abridgement of
Freedoms of the people by gradual and silent encroachment of
those in power than by violent and sudden usurpations."*
—James Madison

*"There is no nation on earth powerful enough to accomplish our
overthrow ... Our destruction, should it come at all, will be from
another quarter. From the inattention of the people to the concerns
of their government, from their carelessness and negligence, I must
confess that I do apprehend some danger. I fear that they may place
too implicit a confidence in their public servants, and fail properly to*

scrutinize their conduct; that in this way they may be made the dupes of designing men, and become the instruments of their own undoing."
—**Daniel Webster**, June 1, 1837

"If once [the people] become inattentive to the public affairs, you and I, and Congress and Assemblies, Judges and Governors, shall all become wolves. It seems to be the law of our general nature, in spite of individual exceptions."
—**Thomas Jefferson** to Edward Carrington, 1787

"A society that puts equality ... ahead of Freedom will end up with neither."
—**Milton Friedman**

"Enlightened statesmen will not always be at the helm."
—**James Madison**

"Liberty is one of the most precious gifts heaven has bestowed upon Man. No treasures the earth contains or the sea conceals can be compared to it. For Liberty one can rightfully risk one's life."
—**Miguel Cervantes**, 1547–1616

"One man with courage makes a majority."
—**Andrew Jackson**, 1832

"Liberty means responsibility. That is why most men dread it."
—**George Bernard Shaw**, *Maxims for Revolutions*, 1903

"In matters of principle, stand like a rock."
—**Thomas Jefferson**

"If we can prevent the government from wasting the labors of the people, under the pretense of taking care of them, they must become happy." –**Thomas Jefferson** to Thomas Cooper, 1802

We can *all* agree there is tremendous wisdom in the foregoing statements from these great leaders and thinkers. The real question becomes whether ***"We the People"*** will glean the lessons from this wisdom and appropriately apply them in time to save our American Republic. That is the question which should daily be consuming each of us as stewards of the American dream.

Chapter Eight

Immigration—Legal and Illegal

Theodore Roosevelt
1858-1919
26th President of the United States
Served as President of the United States from 1901 to 1909

"The things that will destroy America are prosperity at any price, peace at any price, safety first instead of duty first, the love of soft living, and the get-rich-quick theory of life."

—**Teddy Roosevelt**, January 17, 1917
Theodore (Teddy) Roosevelt (1858–1919) was the
twenty-sixth president of the United States (1901-1909).

THEODORE ROOSEVELT ON IMMIGRANTS AND BECOMING AN AMERICAN

"In the first place we should insist that if the immigrant who comes here in good faith becomes an American and assimilates himself to us, he shall be treated on an exact equality with everyone else, for it is an outrage to discriminate against any such man because of creed, or birthplace, or origin. But this is predicated upon the man's becoming in very fact an American and nothing but an American.... There can be no divided allegiance here. Any man who says he is an American, but something else also, isn't an American at all. We have room for but one flag, the American flag, and this excludes the red flag, which symbolizes all wars against liberty and civilization, just as much as it excludes any foreign flag of a nation to which we are hostile.... We have room for but one language here, and that is the English language ... and we have room for but one sole loyalty and that is a loyalty to the American people."

—**Theodore Roosevelt**,
January 3, 1919, three days before he died

"Every immigrant who comes here should be required within five years to learn English or to leave the country."

—**Theodore Roosevelt**

"Americanization" was a favorite theme of Roosevelt's during his later years. He railed against "*hyphenated Americans*" and the prospect of a nation "brought to ruins by a tangle of squabbling nationalities." Roosevelt advocated the compulsory learning of English by every naturalized citizen. *"Every immigrant who comes here should be required within five years to learn English or to leave the country,"* Roosevelt said in a statement to the *Kansas City Star* in 1918. *"English should be the only language taught or used in the public schools."*

"It is our boast that we admit the immigrant to full fellowship and equality with the native-born."

—Theodore Roosevelt

Roosevelt also insisted, on more than one occasion, that America had no room for what he called *"fifty-fifty allegiance."* In a speech made in 1917, Roosevelt said, *"It is our boast that we admit the immigrant to full fellowship and equality with the native-born. In return, we demand that he shall share our undivided allegiance to the one flag which floats over all of us."*

"When he had a 'falling out' with the Republican Party, he formed a third party, the Progressive or "Bull Moose" party, and Roosevelt came closer to winning a presidential election under a third party than has anyone before or since, earning 27 percent of the total vote."

Teddy Roosevelt was president during the beginning of the "Progressive Era" in American political thinking. He was something of a living contradiction. His party affiliation was Republican, and yet he was the president who began big government intervention in society and into the lives of the people in a significant way. He decided that big business was bad for America and became known as a "trustbuster." Teddy Roosevelt felt that private property rights should ultimately be subject to the good of society and its control, and not simply subject to the rights of the property owner who had worked to acquire them. He was in favor of a progressive income tax before we ever had one. He was in favor of setting aside millions of acres of government land for the "common good." Teddy Roosevelt was an activist leader and an extremely energetic person. When he had a "falling out" with the Republican Party, he formed a third party, the Progressive or "Bull Moose" party, and Roosevelt came closer to winning a presidential election under a third party than has anyone before or since, earning 27 percent of the total vote.

"Teddy Roosevelt was 'progressive' and 'liberal' in so many ways, yet he was what can only be described as extremely conservative when it came to his views on immigration ..."

Isn't it interesting that Teddy Roosevelt was "progressive" and "liberal" in so many ways, yet he was what can only be described as extremely conservative when it came to his views on immigration? No one can argue that Teddy Roosevelt wasn't a true American patriot and a protector of our American sovereignty. I would not have agreed with much of Teddy Roosevelt's domestic political views; however, I firmly believe Teddy Roosevelt was "right on" when it came to his approaches and views on immigration.

> *"Most Americans firmly believe in immigration … it is also true that most Americans firmly believe in enforcing the laws of the United States. Enforcing laws is where the real problem resides on the issue of immigration …"*

Most Americans firmly believe in immigration. In a very real sense, we are *all* immigrants by virtue of the fact that none of us have to count back very many generations before we find our heritage or "roots" in another land. Our history is in many ways defined by the concept of the "melting pot," and in many respects our diversity is what helped make America so strong. In fact, many of our founders commented on this after they successfully wrote the U.S. Constitution. They all marveled that they were able to bring together so diverse a group of people and hammer out a document to form a nation that got its power from one single, united people—a uniquely "American" people. So while most Americans firmly believe in immigration, it is also true that most Americans firmly believe in enforcing the laws of the United States. Enforcing laws is where the real problem resides on the issue of immigration, and isn't this really what Teddy Roosevelt was saying in his approach to handling immigrants? *"We welcome all newcomers so long as they become in every way an American. There can be no divided or 'fifty-fifty' allegiance."* We didn't have the huge and pervasive problem of "illegal" immigration in Teddy Roosevelt's day. If it had been a problem in his day, I can just see the old "Rough Rider" perched on top of a 700-mile fence with rifle in hand. Teddy Roosevelt would have been leading the charge on solving this issue.

Perhaps the best way to illustrate how illegal immigration manifests itself into inequities for people and real problems for America would be to compare two families. We shall call them "Joe Legal" and "Jose Illegal."

Gaming the System, The Tale of Two Families: "Joe Legal" and "Jose Illegal"

Both families have two parents and two children, and both families live in the state of California.

Joe Legal works in construction, has a Social Security number, and makes $25.00 per hour, with taxes deducted.

Jose Illegal also works in construction, has *no* Social Security number, and gets paid $15.00 per hour in cash "under the table," thereby paying *no* county, state, Social Security, or federal taxes.

Ready? Now pay close attention as this gets real interesting …

Joe Legal's income: $25.00 per hour x 40 hours = $1000.00 per week, or $52,000.00 per year. Now take 40% away for local, state, Social Security, and federal taxes. Joe Legal now has $31,200.00.

Jose Illegal's income: $15.00 per hour x 40 hours = $600.00 per week, or $31,200.00 per year. Jose Illegal pays *no* taxes of any kind. Jose Illegal still has $31,200.00, coincidentally the same as Joe Legal's *after-tax* income.

Joe Legal pays medical and dental insurance with limited coverage for his family at $600.00 per month, or $7,200.00 per year. Joe Legal now has $24,000.00.

Jose Illegal has full medical and dental coverage through the state and local clinics at a cost to Jose and his family of $0.00 per year. Jose Illegal still has his original $31,200.00.

Joe Legal makes too much money and is not eligible for food stamps or welfare. Joe Legal pays $500.00 per month for food, or $6,000.00 per year. Joe Legal now has $18,000.00.

Jose Illegal has no documented income and is eligible for food stamps and welfare. Jose Illegal still has his original $31,200.00.

Joe Legal pays rent of $900.00 per month, or $10,800.00 per year. Joe Legal now has $7,200.00.

Jose Illegal receives a $500.00 per month federal rent subsidy. Jose Illegal pays out that $500.00 per month, or $6,000.00 per year. Jose Illegal still has his original $ 31,200.00.

Joe Legal pays $300.00 per month, or $3,600.00 per year for automobile and renter's insurance. Joe Legal now has $3,600.00.

Jose Illegal says, "We don't need no stinkin' insurance!" and still has his original $31,200.00.

Joe Legal now has to try to find a way to make his remaining $3,600.00 stretch to pay his utilities, gasoline, and other expenses leaving him ultimately with *no money.*

Jose Illegal has to make his $31,200.00 stretch to pay utilities, gasoline, and so forth after he sends all of the money that he possibly can out of the United States and back to "the old country" every month.

Joe Legal now works overtime on Saturdays or gets a part-time job after work.

Jose Illegal has his nights and weekends off to enjoy with his family.

Joe Legal's and Jose Illegal's children both attend the same school. Joe Legal pays for his children's lunches, while Jose Illegal's children get a government-sponsored lunch. Jose Illegal's children have an afterschool ESL (English as a Second Language) program. Joe Legal's children go home to an empty house because their mother has to work part-time to help make ends meet.

Joe Legal and Jose Illegal both enjoy the same police and fire services. Joe paid for them. and Jose did not pay.

Do you get it now? It's really pretty simple, isn't it? If you vote for any politician that supports allowing in illegal aliens, then consider yourself a part of the problem. We have been dillydallying too long on this important issue. The time has come to take a stand for America and American citizens! *What are we waiting for?*

A WAY OUT—LET'S PUT JOE IN CHARGE

Speaking of a man named Joe, let's consider whether we should put Joe Arpaio in charge of our nation's illegal immigration problem. After all, he already lives in a border state (Arizona) and has a perfect resume for the job. The following is a "bio" taken from the Maricopa County Sheriff's Office Web site, www.mcso.org:

You probably know him as "America's Toughest Sheriff," a name given to him years ago by the media. It's a name he certainly has earned as head of the nation's third largest Sheriff's Office which employs over 3,000 people. But even before he became Sheriff in 1993, Joe Arpaio was one tough lawman. After serving in the U.S. Army from 1950 to 1953, and as a Washington, D.C., and Las Vegas, NV, police officer for almost five years, Arpaio went on to build a federal law enforcement career and a reputation for fighting crime and drug trafficking around the world.

He began his career as a federal narcotics agent, establishing a stellar record in infiltrating drug organizations from Turkey to the Middle East to Mexico, Central, and South America to cities around the U.S. His expertise and success led him to top management positions around the world with the U.S. Drug Enforcement Administration (DEA). He concluded his remarkable 32-year federal career as head of the DEA for Arizona.

In 1992 Arpaio successfully campaigned to become the Sheriff of Maricopa County. Since then he has been reelected to an unprecedented five 4-year terms. During his tenure as Sheriff of Maricopa County, Arpaio has consistently earned extraordinarily high public approval ratings.

With over four decades experience in law enforcement, Arpaio knows what the public wants. "The public is my boss," he says, "So I serve the public." He has served them well by establishing several unique programs.

Arpaio has over 10,000 inmates in his jail system. In August, 1993, he started the nation's largest Tent City for convicted inmates. Two thousand convicted men and women serve their sentences in a canvas incarceration compound. It is a remarkable success story that has attracted the attention of government officials, presidential candidates, and media worldwide.

Of equal success and notoriety are his chain gangs, which contribute thousands of dollars of free labor to the community. The male chain gang, and the world's first-ever female and juvenile chain gangs, clean streets, paint over graffiti, and bury the indigent in the county cemetery.

Also impressive are the Sheriff's get-tough policies. For example, he banned smoking, coffee, movies, pornographic magazines, and unrestricted TV in all jails. He serves the cheapest meals in the U.S. too. The average meal costs about 15 cents, and inmates are fed only twice daily, to cut the labor costs of meal delivery. He even stopped serving them salt and pepper to save taxpayers $20,000 a year.

Another program Arpaio is very well known for is the pink under shorts he makes all inmates wear. Years ago, when the Sheriff learned that inmates were stealing jailhouse white boxers, Arpaio had all inmate underwear dyed pink for better inventory control. The same is true for the Sheriff's handcuffs. When they started disappearing, he ordered pink handcuffs as a replacement. And later, when the Sheriff learned the calming, psychological effects of the color pink—sheets, towels, socks— everything inmates wear, except for the old-fashioned black and white striped uniform, were dyed pink.

Arpaio has started another controversial program, the website WWW.MCSO.org, so that all those arrested (about 300 per day) are recorded on the Sheriff's website as they are booked and processed into jail. Just under a million hits daily come into the website, making it one of the most visible law enforcement sites on the World Wide Web.

In addition to these tough measures, the Sheriff has launched rehabilitative programs like "Hard Knocks High," the only accredited high school under a Sheriff in an American jail, and ALPHA, an anti-substance-abuse program that has greatly reduced recidivism.

As chief law enforcement officer for the county, Arpaio continues to reduce crime with hard-hitting enforcement methods. His deputies and detectives have solved several high-profile murder cases, including nine child murders. The posse, whose ranks have increased to 3,000 members under Arpaio, is the nation's largest volunteer posse. Posse men and women help in search and rescue and other traditional police work as well as in special operations like rounding up deadbeat parents, fighting prostitution, patrolling malls during holidays, and investigating animal cruelty complaints. The posse's contributions are invaluable and essentially free to taxpayers.

No wonder Sheriff Arpaio has been profiled in over 2,000 U.S. and foreign newspapers, magazines, and TV news programs. His leadership and the excellent work of his staff have catapulted the Maricopa County Sheriff's Office into the ranks of elite law enforcement agencies.

On a personal note, Sheriff Arpaio and his wife Ava have been married for over 51 years and have two children, both residing in the Phoenix area. The Arpaios have four grandchildren.

Arpaio looks forward to many more years as Sheriff of Maricopa County.

SOLUTIONS TO THE ILLEGAL IMMIGRATION ISSUE

"Reagan would be the first to say that "killing them with kindness" was obviously not the answer ... There is no reason to stick our hand back into that buzz saw."

1. **Enforce our laws.** No more amnesty. We have perfect proof that this concept doesn't work. It was 1986 when Ronald Reagan signed on to this idea. Were he living today, Reagan would be the first to say that *"killing them with kindness"* was obviously *not* the answer. It was a kind and generous American gesture of goodwill, but the kindness wasn't reciprocated. There is no reason to stick our hand back into that buzz saw. We all have compassion for the plight of people everywhere in the world living in poor conditions; however, that compassion cannot be used as a reason to ignore our laws and, more importantly, to discriminate against those immigrants who are patiently waiting in line to become Americans by following the rules that are clearly set out for them to follow. Allowing illegal immigrants a "free pass" to jump ahead in the line is outright discrimination against those who are following the laws, and it doesn't say much for American ethics or fairness. So from now on, if you are

caught here illegally, you will be immediately taken back home. If your children were born here to you while you were an illegal alien and *they* are therefore also American citizens, you had better have someone in mind who is living here legally to leave them with and to care for them, or you will be taking them "home" with you under their dual citizenship status. Sorry, but using innocent children to break United States laws will no longer be tolerated nor allowed in America.

> *"If we can send men back and forth to the moon and create missile defense systems in outer space, then we can secure our borders."*

2. **Truly secure the borders.** No half measures here. No more unfulfilled promises of starting a fence and not finishing a fence. If we can send men back and forth to the moon and create missile defense systems in outer space, then we can secure our borders. *Finish the fence.* Put high-tech surveillance equipment on the border to monitor every movement.

> *"How can we expect immigrants to assimilate if we make it okay for them to maintain their "old country" heritage?"*

3. **No more tolerance on divided allegiance.** English is spoken in America. Learn it and learn it fast. When you are in public, speak *only* English. In other words, when in Rome, do as the Romans do. No more voice mails in foreign languages. No more product instructions in seven foreign languages. No more press 1 for Spanish, 2 for French, 3 for German, 4 for English. All public signs are to be in English. How can we expect immigrants to assimilate if we make it okay for them to maintain their "old country" heritage? No, let's be clear: immigrants must become "in every way" an American or return to the home of their origin.

> *"It is unfair to indenture our future American generations. America is spending an average of $300 per week on unemployment benefits for each unemployed American. Let's employ Americans in the jobs that illegal immigrants are holding."*

There is much more to this immigration issue than just fairness. Fairness is reason enough to finally enforce our laws and do the right thing as outlined above; however, what we must also face is that *we are broke*. Americans spend billions of dollars in medical costs, education, and social programs on illegal aliens every year. This is money that we don't have and must therefore borrow in the names of our children and grandchildren. But then that's really a fairness issue in itself, right? It is unfair to indenture our future American generations. America is spending an average of $300 per week on unemployment benefits for each unemployed American. Let's employ Americans in the jobs that illegal immigrants are holding. If not, in a very real sense, U.S. taxpayers are paying the illegals' wages.

CHAPTER NINE

FAITH OF OUR FOUNDING FATHERS

FIRST AMENDMENT TO THE U. S. CONSTITUTION

Congress shall make no law respecting an establishment of religion, or prohibiting the free exercise thereof; or abridging the freedom of speech, or of the press; or the right of the people peaceably to assemble, and to petition the Government for a redress of grievances.

"To those who would choose to separate God from America, I can only say good luck to you."

To those who would choose to separate God from America, I can only say good luck to you. Since the early days of America's founding, there has been a vigorous ongoing discussion and debate about the separation of church and state. To me, the issue is not that difficult. Yes, I believe that the founders *did* intend to separate the church from the state. However, our founders never actually used those exact words. Those words came along later as *We the People* were arguing over what the founders intended. Our nation's founders were very clear. They simply did not want any particular religion, church, or denomination to dominate the public debate or to be considered *the* faith of America or *the* faith of her people. There can really be no other way of interpreting what they meant when they spelled it out for us in the First Amendment to the U.S. Constitution in our Bill of Rights, as quoted above.

> *"while our founders made certain that* **'We the People'** *would have Freedom of religion, this in no way implies that they desired that we have Freedom from religion."*

Why do we need to make this subject so complicated? The founders were *exceedingly* clear—Congress would not *"establish"* a religion for us nor would it *"prohibit"* us from exercising our own choice of religion or faith. Our founders were all about *Freedom*. It should also be pointed out that while our founders made certain that **"We the People"** would have Freedom *of* religion, this in no way implies that they desired that we have Freedom *from* religion. The evidence is actually quite to the contrary. What cannot be left open to debate is whether or not the majority of our founders believed that there is a Divine Creator, a God. On that subject there can be little doubt.

> *"To our founders, government's only real purpose was to protect people from losing these 'natural rights' of man that were given them by God."*

Surely no thinking person can make a serious argument that the founders wanted to separate God from America. If that is a debate anyone desires to have, they are about 236 years too late. The founders *all* acknowledged that there is a Divine Creator, a God, by their very act of signing the Declaration of Independence. In fact, there is nothing that the founders desired to be clearer about than our connection to God, our Creator. After all, they put it in the first two sentences of the first two paragraphs of their Declaration of Independence. They then hung their entire right to make a separation from Great Britain on their having been given that very choice to do so *by God*. No, the debate of America's connection to God was fought and won *in God's favor* before July 4, 1776. Our founders wanted to leave no doubt about their collective belief in God. The entire essence of the existence of the United States is predicated upon our collective belief in God and with it our unalienable rights, as given *by God*, to Life, Liberty, and the pursuit of Happiness. When our rights were described as unalienable by our founders, they were specific in using that term, which means rights that cannot be separated from us, given to us, or taken away from us, by anyone *other than God*. They are *"natural rights."* To our founders, government's only real purpose was to protect people from losing these "natural rights" of man that were given them by God.

FROM THE SECOND PARAGRAPH OF AMERICA'S DECLARATION OF INDEPENDENCE:

"We hold these truths to be self-evident, that all men are created equal, that they are endowed by their Creator with certain unalienable Rights, that among these are Life, Liberty and the pursuit of Happiness. — That to secure these rights, Governments are instituted among Men, deriving their just powers from the consent of the governed,…"

Yes, our founders believed in God. One can find evidence of this everywhere. The following is just a sampling:

"reason and experience both forbid us to expect that National morality can prevail in exclusion of religious principle…. It is impossible to rightly govern the world without God & Bible."

—George Washington

"The general principles upon which the Fathers achieved independence were the general principles of Christianity… I will avow that I believed and now believe that those general principles of Christianity are as eternal and immutable as the existence and attributes of God."

—John Adams

143

"July 4th ought to be commemorated as the day of deliverance by solemn acts of devotion to God Almighty."

–**John Adams** in a letter written to
Abigail on the day the Declaration was approved by Congress

"Our Constitution was made only for a moral and religious people. It is wholly inadequate to the government of any other."

–**John Adams**, *October 11, 1798*

"I have examined all religions, as well as my narrow sphere, my straightened means, and my busy life, would allow; and the result is that the Bible is the best Book in the world. It contains more philosophy than all the libraries I have seen."

—**John Adams**
in a December 25, 1813, letter to Thomas Jefferson

"Without Religion this World would be something not fit to be mentioned in polite company, I mean Hell."

—**John Adams**
in an April 19, 1817, letter to Thomas Jefferson

"I have lived, Sir, a long time, and the longer I live, the more convincing proof I see of this truth—that God governs in the affairs of man. And if a sparrow cannot fall to the ground without his notice, is it probable that an empire can rise without His aid?"

—**Benjamin Franklin**
in a speech to the Constitutional
Convention of 1787

"Talking against religion is unchaining a tiger; the beast let loose may worry his deliverer."

—**Benjamin Franklin**, *Poor Richard's Almanac*, 1751

"How many observe Christ's birthday! How few, his precepts! O! 'tis easier to keep holidays than commandments."

—**Benjamin Franklin**, *Poor Richard's Almanac*, 1732

"In the beginning of the contest with Britain, when we were sensible of danger, we had daily prayers in this room for Divine protection. Our prayers, Sir, were heard, and they were graciously answered ... do we imagine we no longer need His assistance?"

—**Benjamin Franklin**
during the Constitutional Convention, Thursday, June 28, 1787

"I have a tender reliance on the mercy of the Almighty, through the merits of the Lord Jesus Christ. I am a sinner. I look to Him for mercy; pray for me."

—**Alexander Hamilton**, July 12, 1804,
at his death

"For my own part, I sincerely esteem it [the Constitution] a system which without the finger of God, never could have been suggested and agreed upon by such a diversity of interests."

—**Alexander Hamilton**,
1787, after the Constitutional Convention

"I have carefully examined the evidences of the Christian religion, and if I was sitting as a juror upon its authenticity I would unhesitatingly give my verdict in its favor. I can prove its truth as clearly as any proposition ever submitted to the mind of man."

—Alexander Hamilton

Patrick Henry was most known for his famous quote March 23rd, 1775:

"Give me liberty or give me death!"

"It cannot be emphasized too clearly and too often that this nation was founded, not by religionists, but by Christians; not on religion, but on the gospel of Jesus Christ. For this very reason, peoples of other faiths have been afforded asylum, prosperity, and freedom of worship here."

—Patrick Henry,
May 1765 speech to the House of Burgesses

"This is all the inheritance I can give my dear family. The religion of Christ can give them one which will make them rich indeed."

—Patrick Henry,
The "Orator of the Revolution" in his Last Will and Testament.

"The doctrines of Jesus are simple, and tend to all the happiness of man."

"Of all the systems of morality, ancient or modern which have come under my observation, none appears to me so pure as that of Jesus."

"I am a real Christian, that is to say, a disciple of the doctrines of Jesus."

—Thomas Jefferson (all 3 quotes)

"God who gave us life gave us liberty. And can the liberties of a nation be thought secure when we have removed their only firm basis, a conviction in the minds of the people that these liberties are a gift from God? That they are not to be violated but with His wrath? Indeed I tremble for my country when I reflect that God is just, and that His justice cannot sleep forever."

–1781

"Have you ever wondered why the United States was so blessed as a nation for so many years and was able to grow so fast and become so highly prosperous?"

So there you have it: America's founding fathers in their own words about their own personal faith. Have you ever wondered why the United States was so blessed as a nation for so many years and was able to grow so fast and become so highly prosperous? Might this have been because *"We the People"* for the majority of our existence as a nation held true to God's simple and fundamental rules of living? If so, what happens if *"We the People"* stray from God's laws? What will become of us then? And have we already strayed? Clearly, that is what Jefferson feared might occur. Jefferson warned us that God's *"justice cannot sleep forever."* He reminded us that our Liberty was a gift from God and that *"We the People"* must never forget this truth. The good news is that even if we have strayed, there *is* hope for God's people:

> *"If my people, which are called by my name, shall humble themselves, and pray, and seek my face, and turn from their wicked ways; then will I hear from heaven, and will forgive their sin, and will heal their land."*
>
> —**from the Bible**, 2nd Chronicles, Chapter 7, Verse 14

> *"allow me to state unequivocally that I, like Thomas Jefferson, consider myself to be as Jefferson said: "A real Christian, that is to say, a disciple of the doctrines of Jesus."*

All of the founders quoted above have made writing this chapter, and indeed the writing of this entire book, a very easy task for me. After all, why make an argument in your own words when those who have come before you have already made the same argument so much more eloquently, convincingly, and succinctly than your own poor ability to add or detract from the effort? I would be remiss, however, if I didn't make known my own beliefs on faith. Therefore, allow me to state unequivocally that I, like Thomas Jefferson, consider myself to be as Jefferson said: *"A real Christian, that is to say, a disciple of the doctrines of Jesus."*

Chapter Ten

WHAT WOULD OUR FOUNDING FATHERS DO?

"A Nine (9) Point Plan to Save America from an Otherwise Certain Demise"

The nine (9) specific goals of *Our 2ⁿᵈ American Revolution* are:

1. To peacefully remove as many of the 535 incumbent members of the U.S. Congress from office as is possible in November of 2012 and 2014, and elect *"citizen"* statesmen, thus forming a *people's* Congress to enact much-needed reforms and changes.

2. To institute sweeping changes in the federal government that include substantially reducing its size and scope over three to five years, beginning immediately with the elimination of the Departments of Education, Agriculture, Labor, and so on (the list is long), transferring any and all required functions of government to the lowest possible level in our society (villages, municipalities, towns, cities, townships, counties, and states, in that order). To repeal the "Obamacare" legislation passed by Congress and signed into law on March 23, 2010 and to pass other measures to decrease federal government spending.

3. To begin immediately, in very early 2013, the liquidation of U.S. government assets, including real estate, vehicle fleets, and all equity ownership stakes in any U.S. corporations such as General Motors, Chrysler, AIG, and Citigroup, selling these assets back to the private sector and using the funds to start paying down the U.S. national debt, beginning first with any and all debt held by foreigners and foreign nations.

4. To call immediately, in very early 2013, for the passage by the U.S. Congress of an amendment to the U.S. Constitution requiring term limits for *all* federal officials.

5. To call immediately, in very early 2013, for the passage by the U.S. Congress of an amendment to the U.S. Constitution requiring a balanced U.S. federal budget each year.

6. To call immediately, in very early 2013, for the passage by the U.S. Congress of an amendment to the U.S. Constitution providing for a presidential line item veto.

7. To totally *repeal* the Sixteenth Amendment to the U.S. Constitution passed in 1913, which allows the federal government to tax individual citizens on their incomes.

8. To put the U.S. Congress and the U.S. President on notice that they are to immediately *cease and desist* from any further "nationalization" of the private sector of the U.S. economy or intervention into the lives and property of *"We the People."*

9. To inspire, educate, and motivate the electorate, inciting them to *thought* and to *action*.

See a summary of each of these nine (9) goals throughout this chapter in the pages that follow. For a complete discussion of *Our 2nd American Revolution*, please read the entire book.

GOAL #1

To peacefully remove as many of the 535 incumbent members of the U.S. Congress from office as is possible in November of 2012 and 2014, and elect "citizen" statesmen, thus forming a people's Congress to enact much-needed reforms and changes.

There can be little doubt that we have seen an unprecedented change in the makeup of the U.S. Congress after the elections of November 2, 2010. What is *not* clear is whether *"We the People"* will replace *enough* of the Congress in 2012 and 2014 to be able to bring about the level of change that is desperately needed in America. This chapter of your book reviews the number of *"citizen"* statesmen that need to be elected, as well as the election process required to get them elected in order to return Liberty and Freedom to the American people.

This goal is #1 because the entire hope for regaining America and honoring the sacrifices of our founders hinges on this #1 goal. If *"We the People"* can change the Congress, then *"We the People"* can change the nation.

"The power under the Constitution will always be with the people. It is entrusted for certain defined purposes, and for a certain limited period, to representatives of their own choosing; and whenever it is executed contrary to their interest, or not agreeable to their wishes, their servants can, and undoubtedly will, be recalled."

—**George Washington**, 1787,
First President of the United States and "Father of our Country"

GOAL #2

To institute sweeping changes in the federal government that include substantially reducing its size and scope over three to five years, beginning immediately with the elimination of the Departments of Education, Agriculture, Labor, and so on (the list is long), transferring any and all required functions of government to the lowest possible level in our society (villages, municipalities, towns, cities, townships, counties, and states, in that order). To repeal the healthcare

law, "Obamacare", passed in March of 2010 and to pass
other measures to decrease federal government spending.

What we now know for a certainty is that our elected leaders are incompetent and that they are completely incapable of solving the problems that confront our great nation. If these people were officers running a major corporation, they would all have been terminated long ago by the shareholders for dereliction of their duties. Well, guess what? *"We the People" are* the shareholders of America, and the time has arrived for *"We the People"* to fire the current management of the U.S. government. The list of their abuses is as long as those made against King George and the British Parliament during the first American Revolution. In many respects, their abuses and usurpations are actually *more* heinous. *"We the People"* will now have to "undo" much of the harm these folks have done to our great nation.

> *"A little matter will move a party, but it must be something*
> *great that moves a nation."*
>
> —**Thomas Paine**, *Rights of Man*, 1792,
> Born in England in 1737—Died in America in 1809

Goal #3

To begin immediately, in very early 2013, the liquidation of U.S. government assets including real estate, vehicle fleets, all equity ownership stakes in any U.S. corporations such as General Motors, Chrysler, AIG, and Citigroup, selling these assets back to the private sector and using the funds to start paying down the U.S. national debt, beginning first with any and all debt held by foreigners and foreign nations.

America is financially bankrupt. Absent liquidation, downsizing, and reorganization of the U.S. government, the reckless actions of our government will soon lead to the demise of the United States through the relinquishment of our sovereignty to foreigners and the destruction of our currency. This is totally unacceptable. Therefore, *"We the People"* will now be taking matters into our own hands. We will immediately begin to put the affairs of the United States into order.

"As a very important source of strength and security, cherish public credit. One method of preserving it is to use it as sparingly as possible."

—George Washington,
President of the United States
From his farewell address, September 17,
1796 Born in 1732, Washington died in 1799.

"Government is not reason; it is not eloquent; it is force. Like fire, it is a dangerous servant and a fearful master."

—George Washington

"To contract new debts is not the way to pay old ones."
—George Washington to James Welch, April 7, 1799

GOAL #4

To call immediately, in very early 2013, for the passage by the U.S. Congress of an amendment to the U.S. Constitution requiring term limits for all federal officials.

Many of the problems that plague the United States of America stem from the corruption in our political system. The most egregious corruption has come about as a direct result of allowing elected officials to remain in office for extended periods and to be bought and sold by lobbyists and special interest groups. Washington DC has become nothing more than a swamp, a cesspool of greed and corruption. The time has come for *"We the People"* to drain the swamp, to clean the cesspool. Once *"We the People"* have swept the majority of our current U.S. Congress from office, the new *"people's"* Congress will pass an amendment to the U.S. Constitution limiting the number of terms elected officials may remain in office. This will cleanse the system and serve to bring the "fresh ideas" that are desperately needed. All federal judges, including the Supreme Court Justices, will be subject to reconfirmation each nine years.

"To prevent every danger which might arise to American freedom from continuing too long in office, it is earnestly recommended that we set an obligation on the holder of that office to go out after a certain period."

—Thomas Jefferson

GOAL #5

To call immediately, in very early 2013, for the passage by the U.S. Congress of an amendment to the U.S. Constitution requiring a balanced U.S. federal budget each year.

In an abundance of caution, as well as to never again suffer the risk of losing our nation or its sovereignty, the new *"people's"* Congress will pass an amendment to the U.S. Constitution requiring that the United States federal government perpetually maintain a balanced budget each and every fiscal year. As an additional limit on the federal government, federal spending shall be limited to 20 percent of GDP. The only exception to these requirements will be in the event of a declared war and then only if the U.S. Congress, not the U.S. President, declares that war. Forty-nine (49) states have this requirement. It is now time the federal government does as well.

"I wish it were possible to obtain a single amendment to our Constitution. I would be willing to depend on that alone for the reduction of the administration of our government to the genuine principles of its Constitution; I mean an additional article, taking from the federal government the power of borrowing."

—Thomas Jefferson,
in a letter to John Taylor, November 26, 1798

GOAL #6

To call immediately, in very early 2013, for the passage by the U.S. Congress of an amendment to the U.S. Constitution providing for a presidential line item veto.

Again, in an abundance of caution, ***"We the People"*** must be prudent going forward in curbing the power, scope, and spending of the federal government. A presidential line item veto will be a great aid in restraining the Congress from their inherent natural tendency to overspend. History has proven that elected officials cannot be trusted as good stewards of the *"people's"* money, for as Davey Crockett said in the 1830s, *"Money with them is nothing but trash when it is to come out of the people. But it is the one great thing for which most of them are striving, and many of them sacrifice honor, integrity, and justice to obtain it."* There is no downside risk to our nation in providing the president a hand in limiting the fiscal excesses of the Congress. Only this measure will bring restraint, which each of us knows has been lacking and is greatly needed. Forty-four (44) states empower their governors with this tool. Our national government now needs to honor the will of the people and provide this for our president as well.

"All men having power ought to be mistrusted."

—James Madison,
fourth President of the United States of America (1809–1817)
Considered the "Father of the Constitution" as well as
the "Father of the Bill of Rights"

GOAL #7

*To totally **repeal** the Sixteenth Amendment to the U.S. Constitution passed in 1913, which allows the federal government to tax individual citizens on their incomes.*

Once the size and scope of the U.S. government has been significantly reduced by the new *"people's"* Congress; a significant amount of the U.S. national debt has been paid; term limits, a balanced budget, and presidential line item veto amendments are all passed, ratified, and in place, it will no longer be necessary for ***"We the People"*** to pay taxes on individual income to the federal treasury. It would be fitting and proper to pass this new amendment, which repeals the Sixteenth Amendment, on February 3, 2013: one hundred years to the day after the Sixteenth Amendment was ratified. This will end, once and for all time, a hundred-year-old battle over the constitutionality and the legality of that amendment.

Gerald Ford, 1913 to 2006

"A government big enough to give you everything you want, is big enough to take away everything you have."

—**Gerald Ford** (1913–2006),
President of the United States, before Congress August 12, 1974

The above quote has often been attributed to Thomas Jefferson; however, there has been no evidence found that Thomas Jefferson actually ever made this statement.

GOAL #8

To put the U.S. Congress and the U.S. President on notice that they are to immediately cease and desist from any further "nationalization" of the private sector of the U.S. economy or intervention into the lives and property of "We the People."

In just the past few years, the so-called government representatives of the people in the United States have piled many times more debt onto the backs of the American people than the United States accumulated during the *entire* first two centuries of its existence. They did this in clear defiance of *"We the People"* as we began saying *no* to their $700 billion TARP legislation. The representatives then started nationalizing entire segments of the U.S. economy, including banking, insurance, and automobiles. Now these so-called representatives are determined to do a takeover and nationalization of the entire United States health care industry.

So: No more new stimulus packages. No more nationalizing private companies or industries. The plate of the 2013 People's Congress is already full of legislation and spending that they must begin repealing. Therefore, *"We the People" of the United States hereby demand that the U.S. Congress and the President of the United States immediately cease and desist from any further nationalization of the private sector of the U.S. economy and that they do not further intervene or entangle the government into the lives or property of "We the People" until at least such time as the 113th Congress convenes on January 3, 2013.* In this way, *"We the People"* will have been given the opportunity to conduct a "national referendum" during the next national election to be held on November 6, 2012, on the merits of our current government's incessant march toward socialism. John Adams reminds us below that Liberty is fragile and that once lost, is lost forever.

John Adams, 1735—1826

"A Constitution of Government once changed from Freedom, can never be restored. Liberty, once lost, is lost forever."

—**John Adams** to Abigail Adams, 1775

<u>*The remarkable lives of John Adams & Thomas Jefferson*</u>

*You read in Chapter 7 how Adams and Jefferson had reconciled in 1812 after being fierce political opponents. Adams told Jefferson in 1812: **"You and I ought not to die before we have explained ourselves to each other."** From 1812 until their simultaneous deaths on July 4, 1826, that day being the 50th anniversary to the day of their both having signed the Declaration of Independence, they gained an entirely new appreciation and respect for one another. Adams' memorable dying words were **"Thomas Jefferson survives"**. Actually Adams was incorrect for Jefferson had died just four hours earlier. However, we can all take great comfort that both men 'survive in spirit' as **"We the People"** go about fighting **'Our Second American Revolution'**.*

GOAL #9

To inspire, educate, and motivate the electorate, inciting them to thought and to action.

"If and when any government becomes destructive to the natural rights of the people, it is the right, and literally, 'it is the duty' of the people to alter, abolish, or amend that government."

We have our marching orders. Our founders, in the Declaration of Independence, were very clear. All people are endowed by their Creator with certain unalienable (natural) rights, which include Life, Liberty, and the pursuit of Happiness. Governments are created among men as a means to protect these natural rights, and the government's power is subject to the *"consent of the people."* If and when any government becomes destructive to the natural rights of the people, it is the right, and literally, *"it is the duty"* of the people to alter, abolish, or amend that government. So here we are—236 years after the signing of the Declaration of Independence and 225 years after the creation of the American government under our U.S. Constitution. Has our government destroyed our natural rights? Let us review and answer that question for just the three rights *specifically* mentioned in the Declaration.

"If the definition of when conception begins had not been known, and could not be determined, then the U.S. government had no right to enter the debate."

1. **Life.** Yes, very clearly, our government destroys life. The grossest example of this is on the issue of abortion. Argue what you will about when life begins. Take any side you like. With respect to our government's action, it makes no difference whether life begins at conception or not. What is not arguable is the action that our government took through the U.S. Supreme Court in the 1974 *Roe vs. Wade* decision. The court decided that *even if* a human fetus *is* alive, it is still okay to kill it. If the definition of when conception begins had *not* been known, and could not be determined, then the U.S. government had no right to enter the debate. Our founding fathers would very likely have said that if the moment life begins could

not be determined, the government should in no way be involved in this matter. *If there were life* at conception, the Supreme Court's decision in sanctioning abortion would frustrate the spirit under which and violate the very basis upon which our nation was founded. Abortions were occurring in America well before the U.S. government weighed in on the issue. The Supreme Court should have refused to hear the case. That is the real issue. We could go on with stem cell and other issues, but these are moot, for abortion trumps them all.

> *"If government seizes five out of every twelve months of the people's labor and productivity, government is guilty of destroying the people's Liberty."*

2. **Liberty.** Yes, very clearly, our government destroys our Liberty. Since "tax Freedom day" is, depending upon which state one resides, in late April or May, we must work *40 percent of the year* just to support the government. If government seizes five out of every twelve months of the people's labor and productivity, government is guilty of destroying the people's Liberty. Shall we bother to mention other Liberty-destroying acts by government, such as their intrusive and excessive regulation or their acts of burdening future generations of Americans with *trillions* of dollars of debt, thereby enslaving them to a life of servitude? Let's not; citing "tax Freedom day" above should be sufficient.

> *"America is really nothing more than a 'forced labor camp' where working people are allowed to keep whatever is left over after the government first decides what it needs."*

3. **The Pursuit of Happiness.** Yes, very clearly, our government destroys our ability to pursue any real happiness in our lives. If happiness means having the *Freedom* to do with your time and your resources what you want, when you want, then working solely to support government 40 percent of every year before being allowed to have any time to claim as your own pretty well frustrates anyone's ability to be happy. Under that scenario, America is really nothing more than a *"forced labor camp"* where working people are allowed to keep whatever is left over after the government *first* decides what *it* needs. Not much to be happy about there. Is there any reason for me to continue? I didn't think so.

> *"If we fail to act, the very Republic for which our founders and forefathers sacrificed their lives will be lost. Is that acceptable to you?"*

So tell me, are you on board with goal #9? Are you inspired, educated, motivated to *thought* and to *action*? So far, we are three-for-three on making the case that the government has destroyed our natural, God-given rights. Is there any need to further continue down this road? Or is the verdict already in? *"We the People" must now act.* The title of this chapter is *"What Would Our Founding Fathers Do?"* Our founders were very clear. Based on their own words as quoted in this chapter, and throughout the entire book, there can be little doubt that our founding fathers would be leading the charge in the second American Revolution. Indeed, Thomas Jefferson would very likely be confused and perplexed as to why it has taken the American people so long to take action. Jefferson reminds us in the Declaration of Independence that it is our right, and more importantly, *it is our duty* to act. A right is something that is optional for one to exercise, but a duty is something you are *obligated* to perform. *"We the People"* have a *duty* to set things right. We have a *duty* to do this for many reasons. If we fail to act, the very Republic for which our founders and forefathers sacrificed their lives will be lost. Is that acceptable to you? In my opinion, we are obligated to preserve our Republic and this great democratic experiment for our children and the future generations of Americans yet unborn. Yes, make no mistake, *"We the People"* are left with no alternative. We are *required* to act.

> *"Whenever the people are well informed, they can be trusted with their own government; that whenever things get so far wrong as to attract their notice, they may be relied on to set them to rights."*
>
> —**Thomas Jefferson** in a letter to Richard Price, January 8, 1789

How Do *"We the People"* Fight and Win the Second American Revolution?

There are essentially three ways to peacefully accomplish the goals of *"We the People."* They are:

1. Internal reform and amendments of the Constitution by our current elected leaders.

2. Election of new national leaders who will reform the government and amend the Constitution.

3. Amendments of the Constitution by three-fourths of the states voting to amend it via a Constitutional Convention.

#1. This first approach is for our current elected officials in the U.S. Congress, under the leadership of the President, to propose and pass amendments to the U.S. Constitution that are desired by the people and further, to dismantle much of the federal government and send many of the functions that are held there back to the *local level* to individuals, communities, and local and state governments. What we already know for a certainty is that there is virtually *no chance* whatsoever of this occurring under our current political system. The U.S. Congress proved this when they refused to support a simple Term Limits Amendment to the U.S. Constitution in 1995.

#2. The second option is for *"We the People"* to organize at a grassroots level county by county and state by state, vote out the current set of national leaders, and replace them with an entirely new set of *"citizen"* statesmen who will pass the Constitutional amendments that are needed and dismantle much of the federal bureaucracy. This approach has challenges, for it is difficult to rally an entire nation of people from sea to shining sea in order to accomplish these big goals. However, this solution is entirely plausible given the current state of tremendous dissatisfaction among the electorate. As was mentioned in the preface to this book, tea parties have been held all across the United States in 2009, 2010, 2011 and 2012. Seven hundred fifty such gatherings were held on a single day—tax day, April 15, 2009. It was estimated that twice that many gatherings occurred again on July 4, 2009. Then there was the march on Washington on September 12, 2009. Literally *hundreds of thousands, if not millions,* of American citizens have attended these events. A like number of concerned citizens attended town hall meetings all across America during the hot August summer of 2009, where they held our elected officials' feet to the fire concerning their desire to take over America's health care system.

> *"The Congress has the ability to render the executive branch powerless simply by turning off the flow of money."*

In our system of government, real change can be brought about in one of two ways—through the executive or the legislative branches. As it turns out, the only hope that ***"We the People"*** have of bringing the reforms needed within the time frame required will be through the legislative branch, the U.S. Congress. The Congress has the ability to render the executive branch powerless simply by turning off the flow of money. Henceforth, this will be our focus.

#3. The third approach is for a Constitutional Convention to be called by the legislatures in at least two-thirds of our fifty states, and for that Convention to propose various amendments to the U.S. Constitution. These amendments would then be sent to the states for approval by at least three-fourths of the fifty state legislatures. This route bypasses Congress entirely but has never been used as a means to amend the U.S. Constitution.

There is actually a fourth way to accomplish the goals of ***"We the People."*** That approach would be by "popular amendment." This approach is actually not even mentioned in the U.S. Constitution. Because it has never been used, it is lost to many students of the Constitution. James Wilson (1742–1798) was a British-born U.S. jurist. He signed the Declaration of Independence in 1776, attended the Constitutional Convention in Philadelphia, and served as a justice on the U.S. Supreme Court (1789–1798). He endorsed popular amendment, and the topic is examined at some length in Akhil Reed Amar's book *The Constitution: A Biography.*

> *"if **'We the People,'** as a whole, demand a change to the Constitution, should not the people be allowed to make a change?... The real issue of amending the document is not in the conceptual realm, but in the practical."*

The notion of popular amendment comes from the conceptual framework of the Constitution. The Constitution's power comes from the people; the people adopted it; it functions at the behest of, and for the benefit of, *the people.* Given all of this, if ***"We the People,"*** as a whole, demand a change to the Constitution, should not the people be allowed to make a change? Wilson noted in 1787, "*The people may change the Constitution whenever and however they please. This is a right of which no positive institution can ever deprive them.*" It makes sense, for if the people demand a change, it should be made. In this way, the change may *not* be the will of the Congress *nor* of the states. The two methods of amending the Constitution that are enumerated within the document might not always be practical, for they rely on these institutions. The reality is that if the people do not support the Constitution in its present form, it cannot survive.

The real issue of amending the document is not in the conceptual realm, but in the practical. Since there is no process specified for "popular amendment," what would that process be? There are no national elections today. Even elections for the presidency are local. There is no precedent for a national referendum. So it is easy to say that the Constitution can be changed by the people in any way the people wish. Actually making the change becomes altogether another story. Suffice it to say that for now, the notion of popular amendment makes perfect sense in the constitutional framework, even though the details of effecting popular amendment could be difficult to resolve. The challenge lies in getting *"We the People"* organized on a national level. While we have never held a national referendum, the time may have arrived to pursue this approach.

> *"If Thomas Jefferson were alive today, there can be little doubt that he would be leading the charge for this second American Revolution. In fact, Jefferson would very likely be telling us that this revolution is long overdue and has been about one hundred years too late in the making."*

Amending the U.S. Constitution, while rare, has been done twenty-seven times (actually only eighteen times if you consider the Bill of Rights to be just one amendment) in our history. *Serious* government reform that falls short of amending the Constitution is even rarer than that, and any *serious* attempts at reform have occurred much less often than the amendment process. As Thomas Jefferson so wisely stated in 1787, "*the natural progress of things is for Liberty to yield and government to gain ground.*" His words would become truer than he or any one of our founders could have imagined. Of course, Jefferson was also the founder who called for a new revolution every ten or twenty years as a way to cleanse the political system and refresh Liberty. Jefferson warned that if *"We the People"* became lethargic, lazy, and apathetic, we would lose our Freedom. If Thomas Jefferson were alive today, there can be little doubt that he would be leading the charge for this second American Revolution. In fact, Jefferson would very likely be telling us that *this* revolution is long overdue and has been about one hundred years too late in the making.

So Where Do We Go From Here?

"this second American Revolution will occur either peacefully through 'We the People' once again becoming engaged, or it will come by staring down the barrel of a gun. The choice is ours."

As stated at the beginning of this book, it is my sincere hope that our 2ⁿᵈ American Revolution can be fought and won not with the shedding of blood, but rather through an active and engaged electorate. I also stated something else at the beginning of this book that bears repeating. It is simply this: If *"We the People"* do not take our nation back, in a peaceful manner by ballot, from the current corrupt bunch to whom we have entrusted it, this does not in any way mean that we will be able to *avoid* a second American Revolution. No, quite to the contrary; this second American Revolution *will occur* either peacefully through *"We the People"* once again becoming engaged, *or* it will come by staring down the barrel of a gun. The choice is ours. *"We the People"* of today have the luxury of a choice that our founders were not given. We can, we must, use ballots instead of bullets. So how do we accomplish our goals?

"it took the states to ultimately give life to the United States Constitution in the first place. A logical argument could be made that we should therefore look to the states to amend the document or to limit its power."

Option 1 (internal reform and amendments of the Constitution by our current elected leaders) is clearly out of the question and is unworkable. Option 3 (amendments of the Constitution by three-fourths of the states voting to amend it via a Constitutional Convention), while never having been used, might be the best approach. After all, it took the states to ultimately give life to the United States Constitution in the first place. A logical argument could be made that we should therefore look to the states to amend the document or to limit its power. Besides, many states have recently indicated their dissatisfaction with our federal government's actions. Several states are already organizing and debating this issue on a statewide basis.

Rick Perry, governor of Texas since 2000, according to the interpretations made by many different people, has gone so far as to suggest that Texas might consider once again becoming its own *nation* by seceding from the United States. On April 9, 2009, Governor Perry said this: *"I believe that our federal government has become oppressive in its size, its intrusion into the lives of our citizens, and its interference with the affairs of our state. That is why I am here today to express my unwavering support for efforts all across our country to reaffirm the states' rights affirmed by the Tenth Amendment to the U.S. Constitution. I believe that returning to the letter and spirit of the U.S. Constitution and its essential Tenth Amendment will free our state from undue regulations, and ultimately strengthen our Union."*

Rick Perry is known as a staunch supporter of the Tenth Amendment to the U.S. Constitution. Below are comments he made at a tea party protest held April 15, 2009.

Texas Governor Rick Perry
Years in office—2000 to present

Governor Rick Perry, April 15, 2009:

"Texas is a unique place. When we came into the union in 1845, one of the issues was that we would be able to leave if we decided to do that.... My hope is that America, and Washington in particular, pays attention. We've got a great union. There's absolutely no reason to dissolve it. But if Washington continues to thumb their nose at the American people, who knows what may come of that?"

> *"The strategy here would be to rally the folks in the states that are represented by the lighter shade that comprises 80 percent of the map and convince the people in those thirty-eight or so states to rally around the causes and issues of the second American Revolution."*

Below is the county-by-county electoral map of the United States from the 2004 presidential election. The shading on the map represents the way in which the counties within each state voted for President Bush and Senator Kerry. What *is not* important about this map is which candidate is represented by which shade. What *is* important about this map is the lopsided nature of the *shades* and what *that* represents. This map would argue in favor of using option 3 for Constitutional change. Why? Option 3 makes changes to the Constitution by virtue of geography, and the outcome is determined by the sheer number of states in favor. There are fifty (50) states in the United States. It takes two-thirds (2/3) of the states, thirty-three (33), to call a Constitutional Convention and three-fourths (3/4) of the states, thirty-eight (38), to vote for and ultimately to ratify any changes to the Constitution. It is highly likely that the map below illustrates some close commonalities among the people in each of the two shades. The strategy here would be to rally the folks in the states that are represented by the lighter shade that comprises 80 percent of the map and convince the people in those thirty-eight or so states to rally around the causes and issues of the second American Revolution.

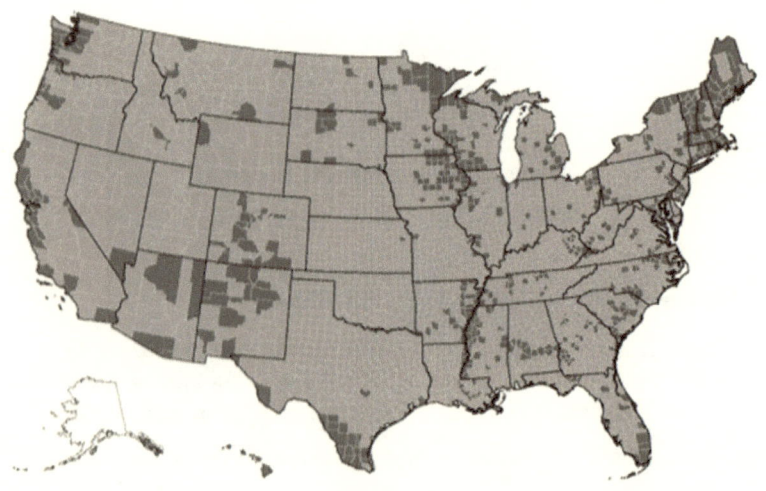

Despite the obvious opportunity that geography represents in this map in bringing about the desired result, it will nevertheless likely be very difficult to get so large and diverse a group of people in each of these states organized simultaneously. This would probably explain why option 3 has never been used as a successful means to amend the United States Constitution. A Constitutional Convention is actually in many ways like the *"popular amendment"* approach that is mentioned above. Another downside to this option is the amount of time that would be required to bring about the change. It can take many years for each of the required number of state legislatures to deliberate and to finally act on these Constitutional amendments. Unfortunately, *"We the People"* of the United States do not have the luxury of being able to wait for five or more years to save this nation.

> *All that "**We the People**" need do to bring about the change desired is to simply <u>not</u> vote for any incumbent in both of the next two elections in 2012 and 2014…It's that simple! We simply replace at least a minimum number of representatives to effect the change desired and have them vote for that change under their mandate.*

If we rule out option 1 and option 3, that leaves only option 2 (election of new national leaders who will reform the government and amend the Constitution). In my opinion, this is the most promising option. Option 2 is promising not just because it has been the only means by which the U.S. Constitution has been amended. Option 2 actually has the most promise because it offers the fewest hurdles to overcome, and it can be accomplished *sooner* than any other approach. All that is required for this option to be successful is for there to be enough frustration, pain, and suffering of *"We the People"* to make it work. And it sure seems that frustration, pain, and suffering are in great abundance in the United States at this particular time in our history! All that *"We the People"* need do to bring about the change desired is to simply *not* vote for *any incumbent* in both of the next two elections in 2012 and 2014. We have already gotten a great start in 2010 by sweeping many of the "old elitist, career politicians" out of power. *It's that simple!* We simply replace at least a minimum number of representatives to effect the change desired and have them vote for that change under their mandate.

It makes no difference if the incumbent elected official is your brother, sister, or best friend, they *must* be voted against. And frankly, if your brother, sister, or best friend were true patriots, they would not even seek reelection in 2012 or 2014 in order to show support for their nation, knowing that their very presence in office would serve only to compromise their objectivity when voting for the changes that 80 percent of the American people want enacted. What is the magic number of new representatives required? That is a question that will be subject to much opinion and debate. However, if *"We the People"* can replace at least half of the representatives in both Houses of Congress with *"citizen"* statesmen who are committed to the principles of the second American Revolution, in my opinion, this would be enough to "do the trick." Why just half, when it requires a two-thirds (2/3) majority of both Houses voting in favor of any amendment to the Constitution in order to pass? Simply because at least 50 percent of the remaining "old elitist, career politicians" will become swept up in the mandate for reform, thereby rendering them powerless to mount any resistance. They will simply remain there as "lame ducks" until they are "term-limited" out of office.

I have attempted to lay out for you a workable strategy to successfully take back our nation. Time will tell whether my dire predictions will be proven correct, and if so, whether *"We the People"* were able to redeem America from what I call "an otherwise certain demise." I recently came across an interesting article by an American patriot, Mark Alexander, that I felt was worth including in this book. It appeared December 17, 2009, in *The Patriot Post* and is titled *"The Time Has Come."* I have printed the article for you here in its entirety.

The Time Has Come

By Mark Alexander

"It is natural to man to indulge in the illusions of hope. We are apt to shut our eyes against a painful truth—and listen to the song of that syren, till she transforms us into beasts.... Are we disposed to be of the number of those, who having eyes, see not, and having ears, hear not?"
—Patrick Henry

The 2008 presidential election was much more than a referendum on the two candidates; it was a referendum on the ability of a majority of American voters to discern between one candidate who possessed the character and integrity of a statesman, and one who did not.

A year ago, a majority of our countrymen were hoodwinked into electing a charlatan with dubious credentials to the highest constitutional office in the land. Since then, millions of Americans who had become complacent about the Leftist threat to our liberty have begun to realize that our Constitution is now suffering an unprecedented assault.

There were those of us who realized in 2004—back when Teddy Kennedy and John Kerry let him take center stage at the Democrat National Convention—that Barack Hussein Obama was a Marxist. Nonetheless, too many of our countrymen were lulled into believing that no leftist politico with such abhorrent extra-constitutional views on the role of government could rise to be president of the United States.

The awakening that has occurred since November of '08 is like nothing I have witnessed since the first election of President Ronald Reagan in 1980. After the economic and foreign policy disasters created by the Carter administration, Americans were stirred to action. Yes, the election of Bill Clinton in 1992 resulted in a conservative takeover of the

House two years later, but Clinton was far more moderate than Obama, and his election didn't inspire millions of Americans to arm themselves for the first time.

That Obama's election inspired a wave of conservative activism is good news.

The great news is that since last November, millions of Americans have joined our ranks.

And the momentum continues unabated.

I knew we were turning a corner a few months back, when an establishment Republican, typical of most such Republicans, told me that Obama's health care proposal "amounts to socialism." This same fellow told me a year earlier that calling Obama a Socialist was just too severe. When I reminded him of his earlier admonishment, he said simply, "*My eyes are now open.*"

If Barack Obama has given us one thing of value, it is the opportunity to clearly discern between Left and Right, between rule of men and Rule of Law. He is the quintessential socialist, and his domestic and foreign policies present a contrast between tyranny and liberty that has rarely been so apparent. Many who have been hitherto reluctant to rise on behalf of liberty or have been too comfortable to be concerned by such conflict, are now making an ever-louder stand.

Benjamin Franklin aptly noted, "*They that can give up essential liberty to purchase a little temporary safety, deserve neither liberty nor safety.*"

Indeed.

Obama is the personification of Leftist philosophy and dogma, and in a turn of irony, for the clarity he has provided to that end we owe him a debt of gratitude.

Despite the fact that the Leftists in media and academia have had a stranglehold on public opinion, seating one of their own as president, which they believe is a great prize, may well be their undoing.

The once noble Democrat Party is now led by those who have turned the wisdom of their iconic leaders upside down.

Then: *"My fellow Americans: ask not what your country can do for you—ask what you can do for your country."* —John F. Kennedy, Inaugural Address, 1961

Now: "Ask not what you can do for your country, ask what your country can do for you."

Then: *"I have a dream that my children will one day live in a nation where they will not be judged by the color of their skin but by the content of their character."* —Martin Luther King, Address from the Lincoln Memorial, 1963

Now: "I have a dream that my children will one day live in a nation where they will not be judged by the content of their character but by the color of their skin."

Today, Democrat Party Leftists deride the notion of individual rights. Instead, they advocate the supplanting of individual liberty with statism.

They promote the notion of a living constitution rather than the authentic Constitution our Founders established.

They despise free enterprise and advocate socialist redistribution of wealth, the ultimate goal of which is to render all people equally poor and dependent upon the state.

They loathe our military and our national sovereignty, and they propose to replace it with treaties that establish supranational governmental legal and policing authorities.

They detest traditional American values, and they support all manner of behavior resulting in social entropy.

Being debated right now is whether an additional 17 percent of the U.S. economy is going to be nationalized under ObamaCare, and whether the rest of the economy is going to be shackled by cap-and-trade taxes in addition to a plethora of other job-eliminating taxes on private sector employers.

Would it surprise you to know that, while Democrat impositions on lending practices are largely responsible for the fact that millions of Americans are now out of work, the number of government "workers" making over $100,000 per year has increased 30 percent since the beginning of the current recession? There are more than 10,000 bureaucrats earning more than $150,000 annually, and the average federal salary is $71,206, not including generous government benefits, while the average private sector salary is $40,331.

Obama and his Democrat Congress have endowed future generations, unless soon reversed, not with liberty but with historically unprecedented levels of debt, which will enslave them to hyperinflation.

Conservatives and liberals can argue various policy points *ad nauseam*, but the question Americans are asking in greater numbers is this: Are we a nation governed by Rule of Law or the contemporaneous opinions of men?

History provides us with repeated evidence that the terminus of nations that are governed by men rather than laws is tyranny. In the last century alone, hundreds of millions have been enslaved under statist dictators such as Lenin, Stalin, Mussolini, Franco, Hitler, Mao, Kruschev, Pol Pot, Ho Chi, Idi Amin, Castro, Hussein, Mugabe, Kim Jong-Il, Chavez, Hu Jintao and others. Who might be next?

Surely not us?

Obama has clearly delineated the difference between individual rights and statism, between free enterprise and socialism.

Alexander Hamilton said, *"In disquisitions of every kind there are certain primary truths, or first principles, upon which all subsequent reasoning must depend."*

Today, more and more Americans are returning to the core principles upon which our nation was founded, which made it the freest and most productive in history. There is a renewed commitment to support and defend Essential Liberty.

John Adams wrote: *"Human nature itself is evermore an advocate for liberty. There is also in human nature a resentment of injury, and indignation against wrong. A love of truth and a veneration of virtue. These amiable passions are the 'latent spark.'... If the people are capable of understanding, seeing and feeling the differences between true and false, right and wrong, virtue and vice, to what better principle can the friends of mankind apply than to the sense of this difference?"*

I believe that a *super*majority of us are fully capable of understanding the truth, if given the right information and opportunity.

As Thomas Paine noted, *"Such is the irresistible nature of truth, that all it asks, and all it wants, is the liberty of appearing."*

Of course, Barack Obama and his liberal lawmaking brethren have done us great harm this past year, and it may take several election cycles, or a revolution, to turn that around. But, the fields are being plowed and seeds sown.

Ronald Reagan delivered an enduring challenge to conservatives entitled "A Time for Choosing": *"You and I are told we must choose between a left or right,"* Reagan said, *"but I suggest there is no such thing as a left or right. There is only an up or down. Up to man's age-old dream—the maximum of individual freedom consistent with order—or down to the ant heap of totalitarianism."*

Patriots, the time has come to choose.

Reagan also outlined a plan for "The New Republican Party," stating, *"The principles of conservatism are sound because they are based on what men and women have discovered through experience in not just one generation or a dozen, but in all the combined experience of mankind. When we conservatives say that we know something about political affairs, and that [what] we know can be stated as principles, we are saying that the principles we hold dear are those that have been found, through experience, to be ultimately beneficial for individuals, for families, for communities and for nations—found through the often bitter testing of pain, or sacrifice and sorrow."*

If Republicans want to regain majority status, the RNC [Republican National Committee] must purge those who have forsaken the first principles of conservatism for power. In their stead they must lift up those who are devoted to the Rule of Law and Essential Liberty, those who incorporate Reagan's charge, and that of generations of Patriots before him. They must back real conservatives instead of arrogant pretenders (see Toomey v. Specter). Short of bold new leadership, what remains of the Republican Party will end up on the trash heap of political irrelevance.

Patriots take heart: Do not wither during these difficult times. For as George Washington advised, *"We should never despair, our Situation before has been unpromising and has changed for the better, so I trust, it will again. If new difficulties arise, we must only put forth new Exertions and proportion our Efforts to the exigency of the times."*

Indeed, the next several years will be a vital test for Patriots and our countrymen. Let us choose to persevere, to make our cause that of all men, to make no peace with oppression.

In 1776, Peter Muhlenberg delivered a sermon, concluding, *"There is a time for all things, a time to preach and a time to pray, but those times have passed away. There is a time to fight, and that time has now come."* He removed his clerical robes and set out to command the 8th Virginia Regiment of the Continental Army.

Patriots, we have great opportunity before us, and once again the time has come to fight for it."

CONCLUSION

CONSERVATISM

The central theme and main thrust in the argument for *"Our 2ⁿᵈ American Revolution"* centers around insisting upon doing what *"We the People"* know for a certainty works and being willing to follow a few specific, time-honored principles which have consistently proven infallible through the test of time. What this boils down to is an insistence by *"We the People"* that our nation and her elected leaders follow and hold fast to the philosophy of our founders and forefathers relative to how America should be governed. What we are talking about here is the conservatism of our founding fathers as it was later defined by Abraham Lincoln. This is not the first time our nation has strayed from the rock-solid roots of our founding. Back in Abraham Lincoln's day *"We the People"* were debating the advantages and disadvantages of following conservatism.

> *"...What is conservatism? Is it not the adherence to the old and tried, against the new and untried? We stick to, contend for, the identical old policy on the point in controversy which was adopted by 'our fathers who framed the Government under which we live;' while you with one accord reject, and scout, and spit upon that old policy, and insist upon substituting something new. True, you disagree among yourselves as to what that substitute shall be. You are divided on new propositions and plans, but you are*

unanimous in rejecting and denouncing the old policy of the fathers…"

Abraham Lincoln, in speech to the Cooper Institute,
New York (27 February 1860)

This quote by Lincoln can easily be borrowed to argue in favor of using what we know works and for abandoning what *was* new, untried and is very rapidly proving to be an abysmal failure. There can now be little doubt that *"We the People"* were wrong in placing our confidence in the policies of a "new and untried", Barack Obama. As a consequence of electing this new and untried president in 2008, the American people have had a front row seat to experience the outcome of his failed leadership. The consequences of a rampant, out of control spending spree, unbridled growth of the national government and corresponding encroachment into the lives of the people, a failed foreign policy making America the laughing stock of the entire world, all has forced us to recognize the Obama polices for what they are— an unmitigated disaster for the United States of America. In short, the results of the Obama policies, which are really just a more advanced version of past administrations, have brought our great nation to the brink of an unprecedented calamity of epic proportions.

It is critical; in fact it is urgent, that *"We the People"* revert back to the old, tried and proven principles of conservatism given us by our founders and forefathers. Just in the past century, a little more than 100 years ago, America began to "wonder off the reservation" toward progressive liberalism. We first began toying with this philosophy under Teddy Roosevelt but then began embracing it in earnest under Woodrow Wilson after 1912. Franklin Roosevelt dramatically accelerated these failed policies in the 1930's and Barack Obama has taken them to a whole new level in America since 2009. *"We the People"* must begin to reverse course and return to conservatism before it becomes too late. Our problem is that time is running short, very short.

We know conservatism works. Conservatism has been battle tested over and over again and has *never* failed us. The most recent and perhaps one of the best examples of the success of conservatism was what occurred under President Ronald Reagan. Reagan's model of lowering taxes and getting government out of the way of the people worked so well that the results were later fondly described as the "Reagan Revolution". Ronald Reagan simply followed what our founding fathers said to do, which was provide for a strong defense of the nation and stay out of the way of the people. This wasn't rocket science; it was simply conservatism, which is also, by the way, being true to *genuine American ideals.* Let us hearken back to the tried and true principles that we know will work and get this ship of state sailing smoothly once again. We have allowed Obama's "progressive liberalism on steroids" to be implemented, tried and tested; and the results are now in. These policies have resulted in a ship of state that is sadly, now full of holes, listing badly in the water, and is one which will quickly head to the bottom of the sea lest we act very soon to reverse course. It is imperative that we move with utmost speed and agility to restore the solid, fundamental principles of America's founders.

> *"If the American people continue their long, apathetic sleep walk through the 6th of November, 2012 and the 4th of November, 2014, it is highly likely that their opportunity to redeem our great nation will be forever lost...If 'We the People' don't begin to take America back during these elections, we may as well once and for all time wave the white flag of surrender to the socialist progressives who are bent on destroying her. This is our moment of truth."*

Time is of the essence. 2012 and 2014 are the "winner take all" elections for America's future. If the American people continue their long, apathetic sleep walk through the 6th of November, 2012 and the 4th of November, 2014, it is highly likely that their opportunity to redeem our great nation will be forever lost. John Adams's prophetic words will then become reality for America: *"A Constitution of Government once changed from Freedom, can never be restored. Liberty, once lost, is lost forever."* This book therefore is a battle cry to you. It is your "call to arms." If *"We the People"* don't begin to take America back in 2012 and 2014, we may as well once and for all time wave the white flag of surrender to the socialist progressives who are bent on destroying her. This is our moment of truth. It is do or die for America and for the fundamental ideals and principles for which she was created. During the lows of the Revolutionary War, Thomas Paine wrote: *"These are the times that try men's souls. The summer soldier and the sunshine patriot will, in this crisis, shrink from the service of his country; but he that stands it now, deserves the thanks of man and woman."* Paine's words are ever truer today in our time.

Some Words of Encouragement

*"**We the People'** finally realized that what little Liberty and Freedom we had left was about to be taken from us with a nationalization of the United States health care industry."*

The first edition of this book was written prior to the congressional election of November, 2010. If that election is a true indicator of the will of the people, and there is no reason whatsoever to read it in any other manner, then *our second American Revolution* is off and running! The American people have awakened from their long apathetic slumber. *"We the People"* finally realized that what little Liberty and Freedom we had left was about to be taken from us with a nationalization of the United States health care industry. That was the final straw, and the American people finally drew a line in the sand.

'What transpired in the November 2nd, 2010 congressional election was just the "down payment" on what I like to call **'A New American Renaissance".**'

There is something very fascinating about what occurred in the 2010 congressional election. What is interesting to note, is that before, during and after that entire process, politicians in Washington, DC and the "talking heads" in the American media never grasped the impact of what that election meant for America. They just didn't get it. What appears to be totally lost on these people is that this entire process is no longer about Democrats versus Republicans. The results of the congressional election on November 2nd, 2010 was clearly about the total repudiation of the Socialist Progressive agenda that has been insidiously and yet very successfully undermining the principles and tenets of America's founding fathers. Fortunately, just as was forecast and urged in the first edition of this book, the American people are using ballots instead of bullets in fighting their 2nd American Revolution. The 2010 congressional election represents a great turnaround for the future of America. Best of all, it sets the stage for what to expect in the November, 2012 and November, 2014 elections which are just around the corner. What transpired in the November 2nd, 2010 congressional election was just the "down payment" on what I like to call **"A New American Renaissance"**.

The outcome of these elections would indicate that Thomas Jefferson was not just an outstanding revolutionary, but also a prophet:

"It is to me a new and consolatory proof that wherever the people are well-informed they can be trusted with their own government; that whenever things get so far wrong as to attract their notice, they may be relied on to set them to rights."

—Thomas Jefferson

It certainly appears from the outcome of these recent elections that *"the people ... can be trusted with their own government ... [and] may be relied on to set them to rights."* Thank you, and may God bless you, Mr. Jefferson.

"Once I truly learned and fully understood what a tremendous gift God gave us through those who have come before us, I felt it my solemn duty to do all I could to help preserve that gift, especially since that gift is under such grave threat of destruction."

Several friends have said to me, *"you must have a lot of guts to have written that book."* Others have warned me to *"be careful, don't forget that you are in business, political topics are 'taboo,' and this could cost you."* My response has been consistent and is backed by a steely resolve. The response is simply that this is not about politics. *This is about America.* When it comes to the future of America, there can be no compromise and no silence. I have learned that there are certain things in life that have a value far above money or favor. Some of those things include holding true to your convictions and your principles. I have also come to a place in my life where I must now work for causes greater than my own. For this reason, it wasn't as though I really even had a choice in writing this book. It *had* to be done. Once I truly learned and fully understood what a tremendous gift God gave us through those who have come before us, I felt it my solemn duty to do all I could to help preserve that gift, especially since that gift is under such grave threat of destruction. Besides, at least nine or ten generations before us have done the same, so it's the very *least* that I can do. Therefore, I don't mind being what Charles A. Beard described as a *"dangerous citizen."* Quite to the contrary, I wear it as a badge of honor. There is no doubt that the course I am undertaking in this effort will lead to confrontation, criticism, and possibly much worse. However, I am more than willing, in fact honored, to accept whatever befalls me as a result of this work.

It seems your author is now officially a "dangerous citizen."

"You need only reflect that one of the best ways to get yourself a reputation as a dangerous citizen these days is to go about repeating the very phrases which our founding fathers used in the struggle for independence."

—**Charles A. Beard**, American historian (1874–1948)

"Our nation's existence is nothing short of a miracle. The United States of America could not have been brought into being by random chance or through some series of 'accidental' events. Our nation's existence has a significant purpose for all mankind throughout the entire world."

Writing this book has been one of the most meaningful and at the same time most humbling experiences of my life. During the research phase of the project, I began to really discover and to understand the sacrifices that our founders and forefathers made in creating and preserving this great nation. That experience deeply moved me. It was this awareness that kept me motivated to finish the book, for I felt an obligation to share what had been learned. Our nation's existence is nothing short of a miracle. The United States of America could not have been brought into being by random chance or through some series of "accidental" events. Our nation's existence has a significant purpose for *all* mankind throughout the entire world. Our creation and survival as a nation has to have been Providential. ***"We the People"*** cannot, and we must not, stand idly by and watch her disappear. If you have been motivated to take any action at all as a result of your experience in reading this book, I implore you to at least, at a very minimum, commit to vote in the upcoming November, 2012 and 2014 elections. God bless each of you, and may God Bless America.

Your humble and obedient servant in the American cause,
William E. Shuttleworth—a farmer from Indiana

"A U.S. Declaration of Independence on July 4ᵀᴴ, 2012"

*A new Declaration of Independence for the United States of America in 2012 is reproduced below using the original 1776 Declaration of Independence from Great Britain as the format. There is a preamble, a list of grievances, and a proposed action plan based upon the current frustrations & intentions of "**We the People**".*

When in the course of human events it becomes necessary for a people to take back their government from an elitist and corrupt leadership which seeks to enslave the people by creating massive debt and bankrupting their nation; a leadership which seeks to flagrantly ignore the will of the governed; and a leadership which seeks to ignore the very Constitution upon which that nation was founded; it is the right, it is the duty, and it is the responsibility of the people to institute necessary changes to ensure their own security as well as the security of future generations of Americans. A decent respect for the opinions of each American, and to all mankind, requires they should be informed of the causes and issues which compel the drastic action being undertaken.

We hold these truths to be self evident, that all men are created equal, that they are endowed by their creator with certain unalienable rights, that among these are Life, Liberty and the Pursuit of Happiness. That to secure these God given rights, governments are instituted among men, deriving their just powers from the consent of the governed and that whenever any form of government becomes destructive of these natural rights, it is the right of the people to alter or to abolish it, and to institute a new government. Any required change must be based upon these principles and organized in a manner to most likely provide for the safety and happiness of the people. Prudence dictates that governments long established should not be changed for light and transient causes. Experience has shown that people are more disposed to suffer, while evils are sufferable, than to rush to change their existing government. But when a long history of abuses, usurpations, and political corruption threatens and ignores the very foundations upon which that government is established, it is the right and it is the duty of the people, to throw off such leadership in order to provide more useful safeguards for their future security. Such has been the patient sufferings of the American people for the better part of the past century.

The recent history of the U.S. Congress has been one of ignoring the Constitution upon which the United States of America was founded. Elected leaders in the United States Congress have been more concerned with their own power, privilege and self advancement than with simply carrying out their required fiduciary responsibilities as servants of the people for the public good. This behavior has been to the direct detriment of the American people and has ultimately led to the threatened existence of the sovereignty of the United States of America. Further, and as important, a persistent and continual transition of power and influence away from the states to the central government in Washington, DC, as orchestrated by the members of Congress, is inconsistent with, and in direct contradiction to and violation of, the intent of the founding fathers of America and the Constitution which they created. To prove these charges, let facts be submitted for full consideration.

The Congress, although recognizing the dangers and corrupting influence of unlimited terms in office and despite passing a constitutional amendment limiting the span of presidential service, have consistently resisted any efforts by the people and the various states to limit their own length of service.

The Congress has consistently proven incapable of self control and repeatedly has reached into the public coffers to enrich themselves with unmerited pay raises and inflated budgets for the administration of their public offices. Further, not wishing to be exposed to public scrutiny in these matters, they have enacted legislation to automatically provide periodic increases in their personal compensation.

In an attempt to alter the original intent of the Constitution without amending it through the appropriate constitutional process, the Congress has applied unconstitutional litmus tests to judicial nominees in order to pack the court with judges more concerned with political correctness and international opinion than with the actual intent & interpretation of the founding documents of the United States of America.

The Congress has proven itself inept and incapable of any self discipline and restraint with respect to their stewardship of public funds, instead filling the annual budget with pet projects designed to provide to themselves job security or to enrich their constituents, family and friends at the expense of the public.

The Congress has exhibited an arrogant and imperial attitude toward the use of the public funds, passing millions, billions and trillions of dollars in spending and running up tens of trillions of dollars in public debt without so much as the courtesy of a single public hearing, much less their own required review, oversight and scrutiny; in many cases passing spending bills without having read them in full or in part.

In violation of the 10th Amendment to the US Constitution, the Congress has repeatedly mandated actions by and for the various states without providing funding to support the requirements, thereby essentially imposing taxes and funding requirements on the citizens of those states with no consideration to the constitutions of those various states which themselves have mandated balanced budget requirements.

The Congress has continually and without regard for the 10th amendment, usurped the prerogatives of the various states at every turn demanding for themselves authority never intended or imagined by the founders of the United States. They have allowed the establishment of cabinet positions and created federal agencies trampling upon the sovereign rights of the American people and individual states.

The Congress has demonstrated repeatedly that they are incapable of providing appropriate oversight of their members. Depending upon the majority party and/or the possible offender at the time, they have either chosen to ignore egregious violations of ethics and the law or in many cases, for political gain, have pursued aggressive unmerited investigative actions against their political opponents.

The Congress has, in an attempt to silence their critics and protect their status as the ruling class, passed campaign laws resulting in the limitation of free speech of their political opponents while at the same time limiting competition for elective office thereby securing their own office for decades on end.

The Congress has repeatedly voted themselves privileges not accorded to the common citizens to whom they are accountable, passing laws and simultaneously exempting congressional members from the force and effect of the law which they have imposed upon the people.

The Congress, in establishing "members only" privileges, often refuse to challenge a members' use of the political process for the advancement of a personal agenda, expecting and receiving in return the same courtesy for their own positions and actions. This "Privilege of Power" is conducted without debate or any oversight, the consequence and result of which is to obscure these actions from public scrutiny.

The Congress has interpreted their responsibility to "advise and consent" to presidential nominees to mean they may refuse the nominee an up or down vote on the floor of the United States Senate when the ruling committee does not wish to advance the nomination, in many cases with the knowledge and complete understanding that the full chamber would vote to confirm such nominee.

The above is by no means a complete or exhaustive list of grievances against the current political class which rule in the United States Congress; however, the list is most certainly sufficient to support the call for our 2nd American Revolution. This 2nd American Revolution is recognized by the people as the only successful means by which they may restore the fundamental principles and original intent of their Constitution and the vibrant federalism their founding fathers intended for *"We the People"*. It is intended to protect the people from the abuses of a ruling class who perpetuate themselves in office at the expense of the well being of the nation and the people whom they are sworn to serve and protect, which was in no way anticipated by America's founders.

This 2nd American Revolution is not to be carried out with guns and bullets, but rather with ballots. It is the clear intent of this revolution against the elected ruling class in Washington, DC to remove them from office in November of 2012 and 2014 and to replace them with true American Patriots, elected as "citizen statesmen", who are determined to follow the original intent of the United States Constitution of 1787. This 2nd American Revolution will restore the unique and genuine American ideals from the time of America's founding and will in the process severely reduce the size and scope of the federal government while simultaneously eliminating the corrupting influences of the current political system. The nature of these changes will, of necessity, not be small and incremental; instead, they will be bold and sweeping, and truly revolutionary in their scope and influence. These swift, decisive actions are necessary and recognized as the only means of saving the American Republic. To these ends, *"We the People"* of the United States mutually pledge to each other our lives, our fortunes and our sacred honor. May God Bless the United States of America.

"Facts Are Stubborn Things"
—John Adams, 1770

Politicians of every "stripe" have enjoyed using the above quote from John Adams, America's second president. I couldn't resist doing my own rendition of *"Facts Are Stubborn Things."*

Fact: Subsidize something and you get more of it. Tax something and you get less of it.

> If you *subsidize* people for being dependent and non-productive, you will find them showing up in droves. If you *tax* people for being productive and hardworking, you will see them fleeing like rats from a sinking ship. Both are simply of function of human nature.

Fact: In 1820, more than 80 percent of the world's population lived in "extreme poverty."

> By the year 1950, that percentage had dropped to 50 percent with very little government involvement of any kind. This was a good trend brought about primarily by a 'spillover effect" of the great democratic experiment of Freedom & Liberty and unfettered capitalism taking place in the United States of America. In the United States, poverty *continued* to decline consistently from 1950 to 1968, and then in 1968 poverty *stopped* declining. 1968 was the year that President Johnson's "Great Society" began in earnest with what he described as an *"all-out war on poverty."* The United States has spent *trillions* of dollars on welfare since 1968. These efforts by President Johnson and the U.S. Congress *prove* the first fact. The actions of our founding fathers in creating the United States of American under our Constitution resulted in a cure for the ills of the second fact. More importantly, it provides total vindication of these brilliant actions by our founders. All that *"We the People"* need do is to revert back to and repeat the principles we now know for a certainty work, those being Freedom, Liberty, fewer taxes and less regulation.

Fact: There is nothing more *"permanent"* than a *"temporary"* government program.

> At least that is until the second American Revolution, at which time this will *reverse*. Once the second American Revolution is waged and won, there will be nothing more *"temporary"* than a *"permanent"* government program.

Fact: **You cannot provide health care to *98* percent of Americans by increasing taxes on *2* percent of Americans.**

Fact: **Most Americans *love* their country, but many of them are *appalled* by the behavior of her government.**

Just since January 2009, the American government, by the actions of American leaders, has:

1. Purchased controlling interests in and is operating the following private corporations: General Motors, Chrysler, AIG, Citigroup, and other banks.

2. Bowed to the king of Saudi Arabia.

3. Told the Mexicans that their drug and violence problems are the fault of America.

4. Praised the Marxist leader Daniel Ortega.

5. Traveled the world apologizing to foreign nations about America's greatness.

6. Offended the Queen of England.

7. Released intelligence-gathering secrets of America despite being warned by the CIA not to do so.

8. Kissed Hugo Chavez on the cheek.

9. Taken steps to nationalize the health care industry in America despite failures of Medicare, Medicaid, Social Security, and other government programs.

10. Endorsed the Socialist Evo Morales of Bolivia.

11. Increased America's national debt more in one year than America had accumulated in two hundred years.

12. Announced the termination of our space-based missile defense system at the same moment the North Koreans launched an intercontinental ballistic missile.

13. Spent $400,000 of taxpayer money flying Air Force One over New York City, causing mass panic of America's citizens, in order to get a photo that could have been created on a computer for $1.

14. Spent $787 billion of taxpayer money on foolish pork projects and called it *"economic stimulus."*

15. Announced that we will meet with Iranians with no pre-conditions.

16. Rushed trillions of dollars of spending bills through Congress without bothering to read them.

17. Thrown a $700,000 party for employees of the Social Security Administration at the Arizona Biltmore Resort and Spa in Phoenix, as a *"stress reducer"* for those employees at a time when Social Security is facing *trillions* of dollars in debt and unfunded pension liabilities.

18. Appointed citizens of America to the very highest levels in the federal government who have cheated on their taxes (two of them actually withdrew when they couldn't stand the ensuing heat).

19. Labeled returning U.S. military veterans as possible terrorists who are "dangerous to the nation."

20. Ordered that the word *"Terrorism"* no longer be used in exchange for *"man-caused disasters."*

21. Appointed thirty-two czars to top positions in the federal government with *no* oversight by Congress.

22. Spent $200 million to buy three Gulfstream jets to haul Pentagon brass and members of Congress.

Is there any reason to believe that these *"servants of the people"* couldn't fly on United or Delta?

Bibliography

Sources for this book and recommended readings for further study include:

Beck, Glenn. *Common Sense: The Case Against An Out-Of-Control Government.* New York: Simon & Schuster, 2009.

Brookhiser, Richard. *What Would the Founders Do?* New York: Basic Books, 2006.

Ellis, Edward S. *The Life of Colonel David Crockett.* Honolulu, Hawaii: University Press of the Pacific, 2004.
Levin, Mark R. *Liberty and Tyranny: A Conservative Manifesto.* New York: Simon & Schuster, 2009.

Hutson, James H. *The Founders on Religion: A Book of Quotations.* Princeton, NJ: Princeton University Press, 2005.

McClanahan, Brion. *The Politically Incorrect Guide to The Founding Fathers.* Washington DC: Regnery Publishing, 2009.

Melton, Jr., Buckner F. *The Quotable Founding Fathers: A Treasury of 2,500 Wise and Witty Quotations from the Men and Women Who Created America.* New York: Fall River Press, 2008.

Paine, Thomas. *Common Sense.* New York: Fall River Press, 1995.

Paul, Ron. *The Revolution: A Manifesto.* New York: Grand Central Publishing, 2008.

Shlaes, Amity. *The Forgotten Man: A New History of the Great Depression.* New York: HarperCollins, 2007.

Skousen, W. Cleon. *The 5000 Year Leap: The 28 Great Ideas That Changed the World.* Malta, ID, National Center for Constitutional Studies, 1981.

Skousen, W. Cleon. *The Making of America: The Substance and Meaning of the Constitution.* Malta, ID, National Center for Constitutional Studies, 1985.

Sources from the Internet

Alexander, Mark. The Time Has Come. *The Patriot Post*: http://www.patriotpost.us/alexander/2009/12/17/the-time-has-come/.

Constitution of the United States, available at Archiving Early America. http://www.earlyamerica.com/earlyamerica/freedom/constitution/text.html.

Declaration of Independence, available at Archiving Early America. http://www.earlyamerica.com/earlyamerica/freedom/doi/text.html.

Erickson, Stephen C. The Entrenching of Incumbency: Reelections in the U.S. House of Representatives, 1790–1994. https://www.cato.org/pubs/journal/cj14n3/cj14n3-2.pdf.

govtrack.us: A Civic Project to Track Congress. http://www.govtrack.us/congress/billtext.xpd?bill=hj111-5.

Holcombe, Randall G. The Growth of the Federal Government in the 1920s. *The Cato Journal*, Volume 16, number 2, Fall 1996, available at http://www.cato.org/pubs/journal/cj16n2-2.html.

Maricopa County Sheriff Web site. www.mcso.org.

Serrano, Jose E. Web site of the New York Congressman. http://serrano.house.gov/.

Snopes.com: Rumor Has It. http://www.snopes.com/politics/ballot/athenian.asp.

Stein, Ben. Ben's House—The official Ben Stein Home Page. http://www.benstein.com/stein2.html.

U.S. National Debt Clock: Real Time. http://usdebtclock.org/.

USATODAY.com. http://www.usatoday.com/news/politicselections/vote2004/countymap.htm.

usgovernmentspending.com. http://www.usgovernmentspending.com/us_20th_century_chart.html.

Wikipedia, the Free Encyclopedia. http://en.wikipedia.org/wiki/Main_Page.

ABOUT THE AUTHOR

William E. Shuttleworth is a self-employed independent insurance agent and farmer from Indiana. Shuttleworth thinks of himself as having lived the American dream. Like so many millions of other Americans, Shuttleworth believes he has been blest beyond measure simply by virtue of having the good fortune to be born in the United States of America. He likes to say that he "won *life's* lottery" the day he was born and Shuttleworth goes on to add that he "won life's lottery" *again* the day he married his wife Linda. Being raised on a small farm within the American Midwest, near the agricultural community of Warren, IN, in many ways, uniquely equipped people like the Shuttleworth family with the ability to know and understand what the overwhelming majority of Americans believe and appreciate about this great nation we call America. There is no "blue blood" flowing through these folk's veins. Born to middle-class parents, both William and Linda went to work as soon as the law would allow them to do so (age 13) and neither of them has been out of work since. Early in life, Shuttleworth earned his living in construction as a carpenter, concrete mason, roofer, painter, and so on. He spent 10 years studying at both Indiana and Purdue University *part time*, where he earned his respective associate and bachelor degrees while simultaneously being employed *full time*, first in the construction trades and later in the real estate, insurance and banking industries. Shuttleworth served for more than a decade as a bank director on the board of the Exchange Bank, an independent community bank in Indiana. Shuttleworth and his wife Linda continue to live on the farm, and just as in the past—now in excess of thirty-three years, he continues to earn his living as a self-employed independent insurance agent. William Shuttleworth is a licensed insurance agent, licensed real estate broker and carries the professional designation marks of Certified Insurance Counselor (CIC), Chartered Life Underwriter (CLU), Chartered Financial Consultant (ChFC) and Certified Financial Planner (CFP).

William E. Shuttleworth
CFP, CLU, ChFC, CIC

Like millions of other Americans, William E. Shuttleworth has been extremely frustrated by what he sees as a hijacking and corrupting of our American system of government as well as our American way of life, mostly by what he describes as arrogant, greedy, corrupt, and misguided elitist career politicians in Washington DC.